MISSOURI RIVER 340

First Time
Finisher

By Stephen, Linda, Robert, Ellen, Christine
and Claire Jackson

For the family adventures we've had...

...and the ones yet to come.

Editor: Megan Linhares
Cover Artwork: Christopher Lightner

DEDICATION

I'm a lifelong St. Louis resident and have traveled by bridge over the Missouri River thousands of times. I am also a former Boy Scout and Scout leader. Years ago at our annual committee planning meeting for Boy Scout Troop 613 of Sacred Heart Parish in Florissant, Missouri, our troop thought of new ideas to serve our community besides volunteering at food pantries and school picnics. "They're doing some sort of river clean up in St. Charles this fall," someone said, "Let's do that." So two months later we found ourselves standing at the shore of the Missouri River next to the Lewis and Clark Boathouse in St. Charles, watching our Scouts pull away into the river with the cleanup crew to pick up trash.

That was the first day I had seen anyone, much less a boat full of Boy Scouts, doing anything on the Missouri River. When they returned later that day with a boat full of tires, plastic bags and an 8-track tape deck, the Scouts were full of stories about what they saw and heard. Any community service is terrific, but we could tell this one would make a lasting impression. The idea of being on the river so close to my home certainly stuck with me.

Ten years later, I'm on the Missouri River in a canoe with my three daughters at 3:00 a.m. on a Friday morning in July, somewhere downstream from Hermann, trying to complete the longest non-stop canoe and kayak race in the world. Slowly a safety boat motored up to us. "How you doing?" someone called out to my girls and me. We chatted for a few minutes, getting the latest scoop on the weather and the barge that was scheduled to pass going upstream later that morning. Then they waved and pulled ahead to check on the next paddler.

As we watched them head off into the night, it occurred to me that they, the staff of the Missouri River Relief, have been the common thread of my Missouri River experiences. Be it trash pickups, MR340 race safety or the Big Muddy Speaker Series, the Missouri River Relief organization has contributed immensely to our community's access and understanding of this unique resource.

With that in mind, we are donating the proceeds of this book to this magnificent organization so they can continue, and expand, their mission: Bringing people to the river with the common goal of improving it.

See all the great things they do at www.riverrelief.org.

Steve, Linda, Rob, Ellen, Christine and Claire Jackson

June 2013

CONTENTS

FOREWARD

The MR340 was run for the first time in 2006. It was an experiment, to some degree, because nothing quite like it had ever been done and nobody really knew what to expect. There were only 15 boats entered. The race was not advertised. The participants had heard about it only weeks before.

But once they heard about it, they *had* to be there. That was the common refrain from all of the participants. *"Once I heard about it, I knew I had to be there."*

Most had never raced before. Most had never been on the Missouri River before. But the idea of getting in a canoe and racing non-stop across the state, once stuck in their heads, was unshakeable. And so they toed the line at Kaw Point. The crowd assembled to watch was awestruck. As the paddlers hovered in the water at the starting line, the Missouri River raced past the mouth of the Kaw. I'm sure more than one person wondered if they were ready for what was about to happen.

What inspires a person to enter into such an undertaking? What is it about the MR340 that causes grown men and women to daydream endlessly, staring at maps and plotting strategy?

Unlike most races which are simply point A to point B, the MR340 is a puzzle to be solved. And perhaps more interestingly, there are infinite solutions. The race is so long and so complex that no two racers have the same experience...even if they are in the same boat! And little decisions like what kind of food to eat might mean finishing a full 24 hours later. A racer electing to paddle past a crowded checkpoint might move up 30 places in 30 seconds. An elite athlete bringing the wrong boat can be forced to drop out by sunset of the first day.

There was a huge learning curve for everyone to overcome that first year. West Hansen of Austin, Texas was the most seasoned ultra-marathon canoe racer in the group. He knew what the next few days would bring. He finished a full day ahead of his nearest competition.

But the rest were learning fast. How to be efficient at stops, what to eat, how to travel light, how to handle sleep deprivation, what kind of boat and paddles worked best, what kind of clothes to wear, lights to use, etc. But they, like most first time racers of the MR340, were learning these things too late. They could only use the knowledge *next* time. While trying to survive "this" time.

Lucky for the newest batch of rookies, this book cuts that learning curve down to a gentle ripple. Inside these pages are insights that will make your first MR340 less painful and much more satisfying. Whether you are in it to win it or are just looking to share an incredible experience with friends and family, there is guaranteed to be something in this book for you.

If you are considering entering the MR340, congratulations! Nobody who has finished the race has ever regretted it. And I've lost track of how many times people have told me that the experience of those days on the water has changed their lives in profound ways. It is a powerful experience that cannot be explained properly in the pages of a book. But a book can definitely help make the experience better. And you've got a good one here in your hands.

See you on the river.

Scott Mansker, June 15, 2013

PREFACE – AT THE START

As you sit in your boat waiting for the cannon to fire, take a look around. The paddlers waiting nervously beside you come in an incredible array of sizes, ages and fitness levels. Their boats range from the lightest carbon fiber kayaks to 30-year-old aluminum Grumman canoes. It might be disconcerting when you realize that roughly a third of this group floating quietly around you won't make it to St. Charles, 340 miles downstream.

You also may be thinking that it's fairly easy to pick out who will and who won't pick up their finisher medals, but in our experience that's a much tougher call than you might imagine.

This book is different than many of the "how to" books you'll find in that our approach mirrors the start line of the Missouri River 340 (MR340 for short). Just as you can't easily pick the paddlers who will finish, we found that there's no easy way to pick the "right" way to prepare for, and paddle, a race as incredibly complex and grueling as the MR340.

In that vein, our book not only goes into great depth about what we bought, what we paid for it and how it fared, but it also explains the rationale as to why we bought what we bought (compared to something that someone else used). While sometimes painful since there's no "one" answer, our approach will allow you to decide for yourself what optimum mix of equipment, training and race strategy may get you to St. Charles. As you'll discover from this book, there's many different pieces that need to come together to finish this race

See you at the finish...Three Boatacious Blondes and Dad

PART I

INTRODUCTION

PART I - INTRODUCTION

A canoe with four paddlers pulls next to a man in a solo kayak paddling downstream from Lexington, the first checkpoint 50 miles into the race.

"So how's it going?" I ask.

"I'm a lot better after getting two IVs...."

It was about then, 50 some-odd miles from the start, we realized we were in a race like no other.

Battling the elements – Check.
Making maximum Ground Crew (including an ambulance) – Check.
Highly focused on finishing – Absolutely!

On Friday, August 3, 2012, at 1:10 p.m., the "Three Boatacious Blondes and Dad" Team consisting of me and my daughters, Ellen (age 20), Christine (age 18) and Claire (age 13), pulled into St. Charles, Missouri, to finish the world's longest non-stop canoe and kayak race. There we were met by our able Ground Crew consisting of my wife Linda and my son's friend Leigh.

So many things went into successfully completing the race that soon after we finished, I started writing down all the different things we did and didn't do to get to the finish. Before long, my short set of notes and scribbling, combined with comments and suggestions from other experienced paddlers, resulted in the book you're now reading.

"But how helpful can this book be," you may ask, "when you've only completed just one race?" In answering I think back to a coaching clinic I attended. Our elementary school volleyball league set up a coaches training session with a volleyball instructor. About mid-way through her talk on Olympic rules for libero substitution I glanced over at a newly anointed third grade girls' volleyball coach and saw a look of total incomprehension. It wasn't that the instructor was wrong; it's just that we new coaches weren't going to get to where she was for a very, very long while.

And so it can be with the MR340. One of the great things with the MR340 is you'll be standing next to world class racers who have finely tuned their approach, their training and their equipment over thousands of hours in order to get to the finish line in half the time mere mortals like us will arrive. The challenge, then, is not that what they do is unknowable, it's just may not be nearly as applicable as what we did, and what you might do, as first timers.

While we knew it going in, it took one look around at the starting line to really appreciate just how many different approaches there can be and to remember there's no perfect answer. So what you're really looking for is the right answer for you specifically that gets you across the finish line.

In that spirit, our book's focus is not to say "this works" and "this doesn't" but instead to identify numerous approaches and their benefits. The drawback, of course, is that there's lots of thinking involved, but we found that as we went through the race, the thinking and analysis we did before hand helped tremendously in making those unavoidable but necessary adjustments over the course of a race this long. It's your ability to think, not paddle, which will get you to St. Charles.

The MR340 Description and Rules

The MR340 Race Rules are straightforward (for a full list of rules see www.rivermiles.com/mr340/rules). You have 88 hours to paddle 340 miles from downtown Kansas City (Kaw Point) to St. Charles. There are nine checkpoints along the route that you must make within a certain time constraint to stay in the race. These checkpoints may also be used as resupply points for food, water, sleep and equipment changes. Sounds simple, doesn't it?

The Missouri River as the course

One of the more unique aspects about the MR340 is the use of the Missouri River as its race course. Flowing over 2,300 miles before entering the Mississippi just above St. Louis, the Missouri River provides drainage to more than a half a million square miles. Made famous by Meriwether Lewis and William Clark during their Corps of Discovery Expedition in 1804 to 1806, the river you'll paddle on during this adventure wouldn't be recognizable by any of the crew that made that journey over 200 years ago.

To understand why the concept of paddling the Missouri River today is so novel, it's helpful to understand how the river was transformed from the time of the Lewis and Clark Expedition to today. The name "Missouri" is a Siouan Indian word that came from the tribal name Missouria. Translated to mean "big canoe people", the Missouria, along with the Osage and Illini tribes, frequented the Missouri River watershed in what is now the state of Missouri. Tribes living along the Missouri River had access to ample food and water, and used to river as a pathway for transportation and trade.

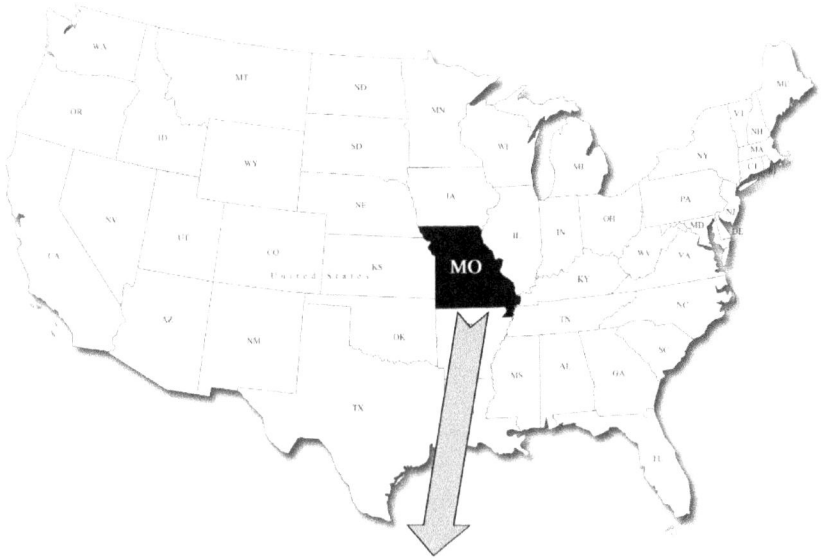

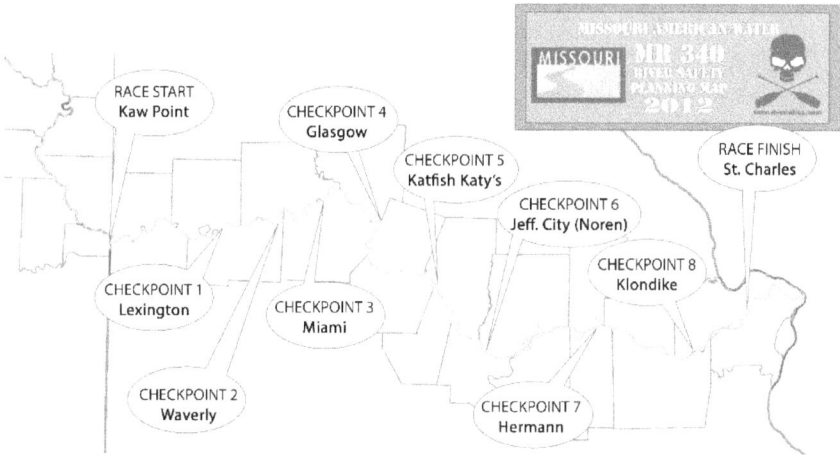

Spanning the entire width of the State of Missouri, the MR340 consists of nine timed checkpoints that may be used to resupply paddlers.

As settlers began arriving, starting in the late 1700s, the Missouri River began to be used extensively to move people and cargo from St. Louis to locations like Kansas City, Missouri, and Omaha, Nebraska, which were staging areas for those going overland to the American west. Steamboats became numerous by the 1830s and reached their peak in the late 1850s, afterwards slowly succumbing to rail lines being built. Hidden trees and rocks along with ever changing water levels were hard on these steamboats, the average lifespan of a steamboat was only four to five years before they wrecked[1].

By the turn of the 20th century, American focus on the Missouri River began to encompass flood control in addition to transportation. By 1912, the United States Army Corps of Engineers (USACE) was authorized to maintain a six-foot-deep channel from Kansas City to St. Louis. This was achieved in part though the extensive use of wing dikes and levees to direct the flow of water into a narrow, deep channel. Meanwhile, numerous flood control and power generation dams were built on the upper Missouri in Montana, North Dakota and South Dakota.

But these dams were insufficient in containing flooding, and by 1944, Congress passed the Pick-Sloan Missouri Basin Program that contained two initiatives: control flooding through the building of a massive set of storage dams along the upper portion of the Missouri, and improve river navigation since the storage dams could provide a dependable flow of water year-round. In 1945, the USACE began increasing the river's channel depth to nine feet, and the channel width to 300 feet, all the way from St. Louis to Sioux City, Iowa. In widening and straightening the river channel, it's estimated that the length of the river was shortened by almost 200 miles.

Unfortunately, something else happened as the USACE fought to contain and manage the river. We as a people lost touch with the Missouri. It started innocently enough. As fewer and fewer people used the river for transportation, there was less of a need to go down to the river. As the sloughs and side channels were sealed off, fish and wildlife were impacted. Heavy industry, meat packers and chemical manufacturers, not usually a friend to the environment and located near the Missouri, routinely dumped pollutants, further forcing away the people downriver. Cities along the river turned their back, building floodwalls and focusing their development inland. I remember as a kid in the late '60s and early '70s that Main Street in downtown St. Charles was a seedy, decrepit place filled with empty, rundown buildings, the river flowing by, unnoticed.

But in the minds of some people the Missouri River was never really dead. There were some men that owned a doughnut shop in Dellwood, Missouri, a suburb of St. Louis. They decided to water ski from St. Louis to Kansas City. This was in the early '80s, when it was a radical idea to be on the river, much less be skiing. But ski they did. From the newspaper account I remember reading, they alternated ski boats from boat ramp to boat ramp, and with lots of help from friends, successfully completed what I now know is a 368-mile slalom ski trip from St. Louis to Kansas City.

And the discovery continued. Cities along the river like St. Charles,

[1]The wreck of the steamboat Montana lies along the shore directly across the river from the finish line in St. Charles.

Washington and Hermann began to recognize the allure of the river and built parks and boat ramps. Volunteers joined together and spent many hours building what is now the Carl R. Noren Access in Jefferson City (a MR340 check point). Missouri River Relief was created to focus on river access and clean ups. And Scott Mansker created the MR340 in 2006 as another way for people to experience this great resource.

These things will be part of your journey as you race down the Missouri. From the trains in Waverly to the 300-foot channel to the camps of Lewis and Clark to steamboat wrecks, their history will be part of your adventure. But you will be a part of it, too. As a MR340 racer, you'll be part of the groundswell of people experiencing the greatness and majesty of the Missouri River.

Why the MR340 is different

Before we get to specifics, it's first helpful to address some of the preconceived notions you might have about the race:

"It's really similar to (fill in your own event)." It's not like anything else you've ever done. We've done hiking, biking, triathlons, marathons, half-marathons, climbed 14,000-foot mountains, paddled and camped in the Boundary Waters, and nothing came close to what we experienced on this trip. Think of a half-marathon. Even on a slow day you could walk 3 miles per hour (mph) which means you'll finish in five hours. A marathon, twice that time. Hiking Mount Elbert, the tallest peak in Colorado at 14,595 feet, 11 hours. But it's very realistic that you, as a first-timer, may be coming up to the Lewis and Clark Boat House 80+ HOURS after starting the race. The duration alone makes this race completely different than anything you've done before.

"There's just one thing I need to do to make it." I'm not sure where we get it, but somehow we believe that we only have to do that one thing to make us successful. Only take one small pill to lose weight, exercise for only five minutes a day to be in top form, read one book the night before and ace the final exam. Not in this race. Your success is based on you and your Ground Crew's ability to get many different things right at the right time.

"You can buy your way to the finish line with good equipment." Okay, here you might have something. Certainly great (not necessarily pricy) equipment makes a big difference. Throughout this book we'll be going into detail on what we bought and why. But the key to this race is knowing what equipment makes what difference, and how the right equipment is just one of the many things you'll need to get to the finish line.

Race Philosophy

Instead of jumping right into gory details about this piece of equipment or this approach to sleep deprivation, we'd like to first start out our book by discussing, of all things, philosophy. This discussion, while brief, will help guide you on decisions of equipment, on resupply, on rest and on all the other things that, when added together, will help get you to the finish line.

The first part of the discussion focuses on why you're in the race to begin with. Is it for adventure? Bragging rights? A dare? Mid-life crisis? Quality time with a friend (or three daughters)? There's absolutely no right answer to the "why," but the key is to articulate it upfront so when you do finish, the "why" was answered, not ignored.

For us (okay, me), there were three reasons. First, we live four miles away from the Missouri River, and it amazes me how people will cross a bridge over it every day for 30 years, and never, ever touch it, or sit on the bank and just wonder about it. Being so close and seeing it so often made me curious. What would it be like to paddle on it? What would I see from there that I wouldn't see anywhere else?

The second "why" was because of my kids. I've slowly come to realize over the years that my core parenting strategy is helping my kids acquire competency. What things can we do as a family that build competency in my kids, whether it's competency as a mountain hiker, as a camper, as a triathlete, as a paddler? Because having competency with those things gives my kids the confidence and courage to build competency in other areas. What better avenue to challenge the competencies they already have, and to build new ones, than a race like this?

My last reason was very simple. I like to be around great people, and there are no better people paddling, at the checkpoints, at the safety meeting, at the finish, than this MR340 community. To be with this group on the great Missouri River is something very special.

So we got a "why" – but so what? Why does the "why" affect your equipment choices and race strategy?

The answer's simple. It's not just about finishing as much as it is addressing the "whys." For us it was enjoying the moment at the Monday night safety meeting where you're surrounded by 1,000 great people all trying to accomplish the same thing. It's making sure the Three Boatacious Blondes and Dad have the competencies in paddling, hydration, navigation, food intake, buoy avoidance and all those other skills that when summed together make a successful, memorable journey. It's about taking a few minutes out on the boat ramp in Hermann in the middle of the night to talk to a paddler and his buddy about their trip. Whatever your "why" is, curiosity, adventure, excitement, wonder, solitude, enlightenment, make sure it doesn't get lost in the nervousness, confusion and focus of finishing.

Race Goals

Now that we have the "why," we can start talking about the goal. Certainly the goal should be to finish and thus achieve the "whys," but many of us have additional goals like "I want to finish in less than 50 hours" or "I want to come in the top five in my division." For first timers, we offer our goal, which was a very simple "Finish Well."

To understand what "finish well" means, it's easier to illustrate what not finishing well means. I'll share a personal example. Years ago I was running a 10k race on a hot summer morning and ended up pushing way too hard for a time that just wasn't meant to be. I came flying across the finish line, stumbled two steps and proceeded to puke all over the shoes of runners in front of me. Besides being not so smart, that experience took a long while to get over and to come back to why I ran in the first place. Did I finish? Yes. Did I finish well? Not so much.

Our MR340 "Finish Well" goal meant that all Boatacious Blondes and Dad team mates that started would come across the finish line together, welcomed by the Ground Team, laughing, happy and coherent enough to understand that we made it. And to be aware and enjoy the camaraderie of the great MR340 community. That, for us, was finishing well.

Whatever the goal, don't let the heat of the moment make you forget the larger picture. For us, it wasn't worth finishing three hours faster if it meant we just "finished." Your equipment, your strategy and your decisions along the way should be approached with your specific finishing goal in mind.

How to finish by understanding how not to finish

What would cause you to not finish the race? Blisters? Heat? Hunger? Dehydration? Sunburn? It's odd to think about what would stop us since we're usually focused on how we're going to make it, not how we're not going to make it.

The reason for not asking that type of question (besides the negativity it implies) is that there can be a million different of reasons that you know of why you wouldn't make it and another million reasons you haven't experienced yet.

While it's natural to focus on what you think it'll take to finish the race, the challenge is trying to figure out the "how." For us, instead of first asking "How do we finish the race?" we asked instead, "How would we not finish the race?" For those answers it was helpful to look at the prior year's race statistics and comments on the MR340 Race Forum.

Race Statistics

Each year, Scott Mansker, founder and MR340 Race Director, and his staff generate a spreadsheet that lists each boat by category, their check-in and check-out times for each checkpoint (see the Rivermiles Forum at www.rivermiles.com/forum/YaBB.pl?board=Race), and their final standings. Looking at that data is very instructive as to where people encounter problems and drop out.

The race you've entered is brutal. Over one-third of all starters won't make the finish line. Compared to marathons, triathlons and events of that type, that's an extremely high percentage. But what really strikes you is the number of "Did Not Finish" (DNF) entries among people who had successfully completed the race in previous years (it's estimated that approximately 60% to 70% of the paddlers in the MR340 are first timers). That's very unusual in that, barring injury, once you've completed your first marathon, you're not just in the mode of completing your next one, you're there to better the time. In the MR340, certainly race veterans are looking to improve their times but at the same time, due to the nature of the race, still run a very high risk of not finishing due to many of the same things that affected us first timers.

Let's look at the numbers. Table 1 – 2012 Participants by Category illustrates who arrived and picked up their entry package on Monday night. Note that packet pickups are less than the total registered, since some aren't able to make the race after they register.

Categories 2012	Total
Men's Solo	141
Women's Solo	15
Men's Tandem	88
Women's Tandem	3
Mixed Tandem	18
Team (3-4)	16
Voyageur	4
Solo Pedal Drive	4
Tandem Pedal Drive	3
Stand Up Paddle	2
Grand Total	**294**

Table 1 – 2012 Participants by Category

As in prior years, Men's Solo and Tandem entries represented a substantial percentage of overall participants. In 2012, these two categories represented more than 75% of the boats entered. Because of the size of our crew, our team's category was "Team (3-4)".

So how did they fare? Table 2 – Where 2012 DNFs Occurred shows at what checkpoint the DNFs occurred (note that DNFs are noted in the data as having arrived at a checkpoint but not continuing onward):

Category	Start	Kaw Point	Prior to Lexington	Lexington	Waverly	Miami	Glasgow	Katfish	Katy's	Jeff City	Hermann	Klondike	Total
Men's Solo	1	6	5	14	11	9	11	1		2			60
Women's Solo						1	2						3
Men's Tandem		3	2	6	6	12	3	1		1		1	35
Women's Tandem													0
Mixed Tandem				1	2	1	2						6
Team (3-4)					1	1		1					3
Voyageur						1							1
Solo Pedal Drive	1												1
Tandem Pedal	1												1
Stand Up Paddle													0
Grand Total	**3**	**9**	**7**	**21**	**20**	**25**	**18**	**3**		**3**		**1**	**110**

Table 2 – Where 2012 DNFs Occurred

What's really striking is that 110, or almost 39%, of the boats starting the race on Tuesday morning didn't finish. But here's where the race data gets foggy, since it only tells you where boats dropped out, not why. Let's dig even deeper. Since Men's Solo and Tandem Teams represented a substantial number of the entries, Table 3 – Percent DNFs by Category converts these numbers into percentages.

Category	Percent DNF
Men's Solo	43%
Women's Solo	20%
Men's Tandem	40%
Women's Tandem	0%
Mixed Tandem	33%
Team (3-4)	19%
Voyageur	25%
Solo Pedal Drive	25%
Tandem Pedal Drive	33%
Stand Up Paddle	0%

Table 3 – Percent DNF by Category

As you can see, the highest percentage of DNFs occurs within the Men's Solo and Tandem categories.

Lastly, how did the finishing teams fare? Table 4 – 2012 Finishing Times by Category shows when the teams arrived in St. Charles.

What's notable about this chart is how dispersed all the categories are across the finishing times. There's no one single category that dominated a particular finish time.

I suspect you're thinking, "This is all interesting, but how does it get me across the finish line?" As mentioned earlier, the MR340 is an absolutely brutal race with an incredibly high DNF rate. So how do you improve your chances of finishing? It's easy. Based on the statistics all you need to do is two things: Be female and make it to Jefferson City.

Bear with me for a few minutes and follow my logic. Men's Solo and Tandem paddlers are twice as likely to not finish as women. Furthermore, over the last five years, not one Women's Tandem crew has DNFed. So they evidently have something going with those percentages, but if you're a man like me, you're not going to be a woman any time soon. So the key is to emulate those things that give the female competitors an edge.

	Clock Time	Elapsed Hours	Men's Solo	Men's Tandem	Mixed Tandem	Solo Pedal Drive	SUP	Tandem Pedal	Team (3-4)	Voyageur	Women's Solo	Women's Tandem	Total
Thursday AM	12	40								1			1
	1	41							1				1
	2	42											0
	3	43											0
	4	44		1									1
	5	45			1								1
	6	46	1										1
	7	47							1		1		2
	8	48											0
	9	49	1	1						1			3
	10	50								1			1
	11	51											0
Thursday PM	12	52											0
	1	53											0
	2	54	2	1	1				1				5
	3	55											0
	4	56	1	2									3
	5	57		2							1		3
	6	58		1									1
	7	59	2										2
	8	60	2	2								1	5
	9	61	1	1									2
	10	62	3		1								4
	11	63	3		1				1		1		6

	Clock Time	Elapsed Hours	Men's Solo	Men's Tandem	Mixed Tandem	Solo Pedal Drive	SUP	Tandem Pedal	Team (3-4)	Voyageur	Women's Solo	Women's Tandem	Total
Friday AM	12	64	1	1		1							3
	1	65	1	1					1				3
	2	66	1	2				1	1				5
	3	67	3	1			1						5
	4	68	2	2					1				5
	5	69	2	1					2				5
	6	70	1			1							2
	7	71	1										1
	8	72	1	2	1								4
	9	73	1	2									3
	10	74		3									3
	11	75	4						1		1		6
Friday PM	12	76	4	3	2						3		12
	1	77	1	3				1	1		1	1	8
	2	78	7	2					1				10
	3	79	5	3							2		10
	4	80	3	3					1				7
	5	81	1	4	2	1							8
	6	82	12	1	2						1	1	17
	7	83	1	3									4
	8	84	5				1						6
	9	85		2	1								3
	10	86		2									2
	11	87	7								1		8
	12	88	1	1									2
	Total		81	53	12	3	2	2	13	3	12	3	184

Table 4 – 2012 Finishing Times by Category

But what about Jefferson City? Oddly enough, although I didn't plot the data until much later, the DNF drop off at Jefferson City and beyond closely aligned with our race strategy. Our thinking was, "If we get to Jefferson City, we're there!" Unfortunately, my strategy had more to do with the fact that we had paddled the river between Hermann and St. Charles before, so it was more of a home field advantage as opposed to some sort of statistical edge. Whatever the strategy, make it to Jefferson City and your odds in completing the race will greatly improve.

Based on the above data, we struggled to put context around all the different pieces that must go together to finish. There's many different ways, but the approach we took leverages the race's results and segments them into the following:

Be Safe – No matter where you're at on the river, not being safe through proper equipment or procedures is a sure way to not finish.

Endure – Know what equipment and approach is needed to make it to Jefferson City and plan accordingly.

Clock Management - You can be safe and endure, and still DNF. How? By not completing the race in the allotted 88 hours. Don't overlook the necessity of staying ahead of the clock.

Successfully address these three areas, and you're well on your way to finishing as a first timer.

Accumulated Advantages

Do you have to do everything listed in this book to finish? Absolutely not. Will you need to do many of these things to successfully complete the race? Absolutely. But which things must you do in order to finish and which ones can you ignore?

Unfortunately you won't find that "Top Ten" list in this book for the very reason that you could do those 10 things perfectly and still not finish because of something else. So instead of providing "do this and don't do that" lists, we recommend the concept of accumulated advantages. As an example, being protected from the sun gives you an advantage as you paddle for four days. Being protected from the sun and paddling an efficient boat give you an even bigger advantage. Being protected from the sun, paddling an efficient boat and having a Ground Crew is an even bigger advantage. Could you successfully complete the race without doing any one of these things? Sure, but every one you don't do is one less advantage you have towards finishing.

Successful finishing comes down to making sure your accumulated advantages are greater than your incremental disadvantages (i.e. sunburn, heavy boat, no Ground Crew). So your approach to this book shouldn't be "I need to do these three things." Instead it should be "Doing this and that gives me an advantage. If I don't do this other thing, what else could I do to make up for it?" Have enough accumulated advantages and you'll have a better chance to make it.

Why did we make it? What additive advantages did we have that others might not that helped us through to the finish line? We used four key advantages that we intertwined throughout everything we planned and did.

Ground Crew

Ground Crews are a powerful advantage. Their role in this race was much more than holding warm-up sweats and cheering. Can you paddle the race without one? Absolutely. But as a first-timer, those things a Ground Crew does, like re-supply, assess, analyze, cajole, hydrate, feed and do Walmart runs, are things that are awfully hard to do from the boat. For us, to know we had someone at the next checkpoint, ready to get anything we need and help in any way, was an incredible advantage, not only from the physical sense of providing pizza and soda, but from the peace of mind it gave us knowing that if something happened, we had to make it to the next checkpoint and our magnificent Ground Crew would find a way to get us up and running again.

Note: We used the Ground Crew Guide authored by Heidi Scroggins and made available for free on the Rivermiles Forum (www.rivermiles.com/forum/Attachments/Support_Crew_Ideas_Only.pdf). Because of this guide's availability and its outstanding content, the focus of our book is on the paddler, not the Ground Crew, although we do discuss in detail many of the activities the Ground Crew performs in supporting the race.

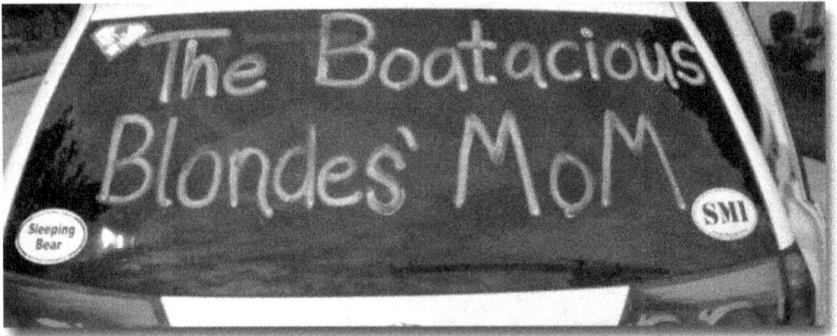

Although most drivers didn't understand our slogan, our Ground Crew van was a familiar site at the checkpoints. Note the MR340 decal in the upper left.

Weight

Weight, or lack of it, is also a powerful additive advantage. Weight is a spirit-crushing parasite that, if ignored, will suck the life out of you each and every mile you paddle. Being smart about weight is not about what a particular item or piece of equipment weighs. It's the aggressive approach of assessing each and every item that goes into your boat with three questions:

1) Is the weight of this item offset by its value during the race?

2) Are there lighter alternatives or are there ways to repurpose equipment already on board so we don't have to take both?

3) Is this something we need the whole time, or can the Ground Crew hand it to us when we need it, then can we hand it back when we're done?

People gather things for a vacation trip without any consideration of weight with the intent on minimizing it as they pack (until they get to the airline check-in counter). What usually happens in a boat race is people get so caught up in everything else that the first time they start thinking about weight is 30 miles in when things start to feel heavy. By then it's getting too late to make adjustments. Don't think about weight just once or twice while you're preparing but all the time. For every item you bring on the boat, know its weight, know its value relative to its weight, and know you're carrying it at that specific moment because you need it during that segment of the race.

You don't have to wait for the race to confirm that you're light enough. Taking a training run with all your equipment is a good way to experience how all those small items affect your total weight and to evaluate your equipment's usefulness under race conditions.

Organization

Success in paddling this race is comprised of lots of pieces, and the better you keep track of those pieces, the better chance they'll be available when you need them. Oftentimes when you mention the word "organized," people envision some sort of massive, inflexible dissertation, when really it just needs to be something very simple that fits your style. For us, I kept a 3-ring binder of all the information we pulled together for the race. That way everything was in one spot so we didn't have to go searching any time we needed to refer to something. By race time, this one binder morphed into a second one for the Ground Crew that contained maps, checkpoint information and other Ground Crew-focused information. Everything the Ground Crew needed was put in their binder before we left, so there weren't any last minute verbal instructions that might have been missed.

The other half of our organization approach was to make lists. I'm a list maker by nature and kept running lists for everything from projected speed between checkpoints to what to put into the nighttime compression bag. Using lists is a great way to keep track of what's left to do and what's been done (see Part VII Equipment and Part VIII Cost for the lists we used). What helped immensely was that most of the lists weren't even ours but ones that were developed by other racers and posted for everyone's use on the Rivermiles Forum. There's lots of thinking going on concerning this race. Make sure you're looking at the forum on a regular basis so you're not wasting time creating a list that someone else has already built.

Discipline

When my son and I went to Philmont Scout Ranch in New Mexico (a Boy Scout high adventure backpacking camp) one summer, I was struck by how differently many of the Scouts fared during their trip. Some looked spectacular, full of energy and enthusiasm after eight days on the trail. Others looked like death warmed over, wet, smelly, cranky, whiney, all after just two days. All had the proper training and equipment, and while some were stronger physically, I saw just as many bigger Scouts sucking air as smaller ones, so what made the difference?

It finally occurred to me as I sat and watched our Scouts having fun playing their daily game of hacky sack. While almost all of the Scouts at Philmont knew what was supposed to be done, our team had the discipline to do what had to be done at the time it was needed to be done. As a result, our Scouts had a great trip and got in some quality hack sack as well.

You, by virtue of reading this book, looking at the Rivermiles Forum and finding answers to all those questions, are demonstrating a key ingredient in how to successfully finish the MR340. But what brings everything together is the discipline to do what needs to be done at the time it needs to be done.

PART II

BE SAFE

PART II – BE SAFE

It happened late in the afternoon on the second day, 33 hours into the race. We were just rounding the bend at the downstream end of Lisbon Bottoms when we heard a low rumble coming upriver towards us. As it rounded the bend we could see instantly it was a big cruiser, moving at high speed and throwing a massive wake behind her.

Thinking it would pass to our left on the inside portion of the channel, we hurriedly paddled to the far right, trying to put as much distance between us and the cruiser as possible. But there was very little room between the buoys and the bank.

About the time we realized how squeezed we were going to be and how bad the wave reflections off the bank might get, we saw that Captain Ahab wasn't aiming for the inside but was instead heading to the outside of the channel right toward us. I made a quick command decision and yelled at Ellen to cut the other direction, and we all paddled mightily to get out of the cruiser's way. We almost made it to the other side of the channel when the boat screamed past us, now on our right, still at full throttle.

Seeing the huge waves come crashing toward us, Ellen expertly pivoted our boat at the last second, meeting the waves bow first at a slight angle. I was too busy paddling to tell, but Christine said the waves were high enough to come over the top of the canoe's bow.

Keeping well balanced and in control, we rode out the line of waves, breathing a sigh of relief that we stayed upright as the last big wave rolled roughly underneath us.

Total elapsed time: Less than 40 seconds.

I thought I understood safety, but encounters like this help me realize just how significant a role safety plays in this race.

"Think Safety"

Walk around any manufacturing facility and you'll see those "Think Safety" signs all around. You might think all the workers "Think Safety," but look deeper and you'll realize those signs are but the tip of the iceberg of all the different things done to keep employees safe. From the use of safety goggles to the well-lit work environment to the height of the machinery, "Think Safety" is comprised of many different tools, processes and procedures that when combined together result in a safer (although not a completely safe) environment.

Whether in a manufacturing facility or on the river, safety's not a "thing" that gets packed in a bag and carried around. Being safe during the race is a combination of approaches, equipment and recovery plans that need to be part of your overall race strategy. Your safety's far too important to add it in as an afterthought.

Of course, you'll never be completely safe on the river, but then again you're never completely safe anywhere. Be it driving on the highway to work, cooking in the kitchen or skydiving, all activities have inherent risk. "Think Safety" on the Missouri River uses the same approach as "Think Safety" for other activities. By rigorously implementing safety approaches, you can be safe enough (and feel comfortable enough to bring three daughters).

But safety is more than just you. As a race participant, you're a critical piece of the MR340 safety equation. Besides yourself, you have additional safety responsibilities for your team of paddlers and Ground Crew, other race participants and, finally, the race itself.

Personal Safety

Being safe as an individual is comprised of two parts: Awareness and attitude. Awareness is the understanding of how your surroundings contribute to unsafe conditions; attitude is how you mentally approach those potential issues.

For me, when discussing safety awareness, car racing comes to mind. One year, some friends and I got tickets to the Indy 500. For those familiar with the Indy 500, we got grandstand seating on the inside of Turn 3 where newbies like us get their first tickets.

We watched the first 100 laps or so and then decided to wander around the infield (which is itself another adventure). When we got back to our seats an hour later, we looked across the track to the stands on the outside of the turn, and there was this empty hole in the throng of people. It looked odd since the one thing about the Indy 500 is there's usually not an empty space to be found because there are so many people there.

When my buddy made a comment to me about it, a fan sitting next to us said, "Man, you missed it, car XXX came in to the turn too fast and bumped car YYY, tore its tire off and threw it into the stands. It hit three people then bounced a quarter mile into the field outside the track. I think one guy in the stands died…."

Huh?

That's when I realized I was sorely lacking Indy 500 safety awareness. It certainly never occurred to me that I could be killed just watching, especially not by a flying tire. I'll also bet the guy who was killed wasn't thinking that when he sat down in his seat at the start of the race.

So what does the Indy 500 have to do with the MR340? Actually they're quite similar when it comes to safety awareness. Those safety decisions are based on the fact that you are aware of the safety issue in the first place and have that knowledge early enough so you have time to make informed adjustments.

Think of our seating at the Indy 500. The inside turn is usually safer than the outside turn since flying racecar parts tend to be thrown to the outside. It's also safer to sit lower, behind the track fencing rather than above. Unfortunately, seating selections for the Indy 500 are made months in advance, so that if getting tattooed by a tire is a concern, that decision has to be made months in advance, not the day of the race.

But note that being aware of safety concerns doesn't necessarily mean that you have to do something about it. Back to the Turn 3 discussion, people sit up high on the outside of Turn 3 because it gives them a great vantage point to see the race cars coming up the straight away into Turn 3, slow down in the turn, then roar down the straight away into Turn 4. For some, the decision is "I'm here to see a great race, and since flying objects are relatively rare, I'm willing to trade off good seats for the very slight chance that I might get hit." For that fan, exchanging some degree of safety for a better view is a good trade off.

The important part is they amassed enough insight into the safety risks to make intelligent choices. Meanwhile, it's very possible that the person sitting next to them isn't even aware that they made a choice in the first place, much less that it involves dodging flying tires.

While there's safety awareness parallels between the Indy and the MR340, what's unique about the MR340 is just how many decisions have to be made within the context of safety and how you need awareness to make choices in the first place.

At the Indy 500, besides where to sit and how to incorporate your desire to drink (i.e. do you get a designated driver, or stop drinking with 50 laps to go?), there's not all that many life threatening safety decisions.

Not so for the MR340. Think of the decisions you will need to make. What's the best type boat to use that matches my skill level but also give me a chance against Captain Ahab? What's the best way to hydrate? Should we sleep on Hills Island or keep going? What should we do about the fog downstream from Hermann? Should I have my Ground Crew meet me in Miami at 2:30 a.m. or should they get some rest? The questions go on and on but all need to be addressed within the context of safety.

So got it, be aware. But how?

One of the coolest parts about the MR340 is that you're following the footsteps of the Lewis and Clark expedition. Traversing up the Missouri

River in 1804 and returning in 1806, they carried everything at the start that had to last for two years. I often wondered exactly how those explorers knew what to do and what to bring on their journey that would get them there and back safely. The answer is that all were accomplished outdoorsmen, and based on their years of wilderness experience they were able to select equipment and make educated decisions along the way.

Not so for our team. While we had a fair amount of experience in the outdoors, it was nowhere near what I thought we needed for this race. Lucky for us there's now an easier way to get more experience, or at least the knowledge that experience brings: The Internet.

By virtue of the MR340 being run now for more than seven years, there's literally thousands of discussion threads on the Rivermiles Forum (www.rivermiles.com/forum/) covering everything from river water levels to best kinds of lip balm. While not necessarily in any type of order, this and other paddler forums do a great job in making you aware of the river and all its complexity.

Your approach to these sites should be different than doing a typical homework assignment. The instructions for my daughter Claire's homework paper may be "Explain how Ulysses S. Grant's prior experience prepared him for the Civil War." From there she would go look at Wikipedia, get Grant's early experience and start writing.

But with paddlers' forums, there's no basic question to answer per se. What you're really doing is wandering around and amassing experiences from many others to develop awareness. You might read about someone's canoe journey from Omaha which then points you to a discussion on boat types which then leads you in to a discussion on capsizing, all the while gleaning their experiences about what happened and why. But if that sounds random, it's not and here's why.

I worry about making this race seem so complicated when really it's a simple race with an unlimited number of approaches. Even with as much detail as they provide, books like this one can only give the broad strokes on what the race is truly about. What you're doing with the Internet is painting in those details that may have been missed or need expanding. After a while you'll know enough about capsizing to form a decision, and you'll move on to other areas like sleep or rain gear or paddles or….

Does improving your awareness ever end? Never.

I guarantee world class competitors are doing the same thing you'll be doing, scouring the Internet forums and articles for information that give them one more edge on their competition and making them safer in the process.

The other part of the awareness process that can't be emphasized enough is training. Some will spend hundreds of hours training for the race. Others, like us, will train much less but use information gathered from the web to supplement the training experiences. While the training durations will differ widely, quality paddling time out on the river goes a long way in connecting what you read with the experience of facing it in person.

You'll have one last awareness tune up at the Monday night mandatory safety meeting. There, Scott and his staff will cover everything from checkpoint procedures to weather forecasts. But make sure you bring along a pen and paper (which we didn't do), because they'll also point out places on the river (by mile marker) where there's dredging or moored barges or other things paddlers need to be aware of. Having it written down would have lessened some of my anxiety and save me from mumbling to myself for 77 hours that "I think they said there was a moored barge around here somewhere."

Here we are pulling into Waverly Tuesday night. The picture was shot facing upstream, west towards the sunset. The cool of the evening was a welcome relief from the brutal heat earlier that day.

Now that you're cognizant of safety and you've done research to improve your understanding of the river, there's still one last thing you can do to improve your awareness.

Ask questions.

Most of us think about asking questions during preparation, and while that's an important phase, it doesn't end when the cannon goes off. It's just as important to ask questions during the race. For us, I made it a habit to ask questions like these at each of the checkpoints:

"How deep is it here?" (So we didn't hop out of the boat in 10 feet of water.)

"How's the weather looking?"

"Anything on the next stretch we need to look for?"

"Any barges coming?"

Note that you're not asking, "Where's the next checkpoint?" or "What time's the cutoff?" since that's on the safety card you're already carrying. The race officials do a magnificent job keeping the paddlers informed, but they're hoping you already know some answers. That said, they're there to help, so if you have specific questions, make sure you ask.

So you've done your homework and are aware of most of the risks you'll encounter. You've incorporated ways to minimize these potential safety issues through equipment and strategy. But since you can only minimize, not eliminate, these safety risks, what you'll need now is a way to assess safety situations as you go through the race. The tricky part here is that there's no perfect answer. Sure, some are cut and dry "I will pull over if there's a tornado" but most others aren't that clear cut.

For us, instead of trying to figure out all the potential safety issues and what we'd do about each one, we instead worked with the attitude about race safety that is summed up very succinctly in the following phrase:

"It's just a race."

Seeing those words will make some shout "heresy." "It's not just a race," they'll say, "it's a life-changing challenge that needs to be finished at all costs!" And while they would be right on the life-changing part, I disagree about the part about "at all costs."

There's something very deep inside of us that drives us to do things like the MR340. It's something I don't pretend to comprehend, but at that same time I accept it for what it is – the need for adventure. There's always been a tendency to romanticize these adventures in such a way that to complete them becomes all consuming; to do anything less would be an unfaceable, horrific failure. Part of it is the focus on success, part of it is the motivation to make the finish line. But there can come a point in time where that fixation on finishing puts life or health in serious jeopardy.

Everyone's different; everyone has their own thoughts and desires. But whatever yours are, realize that decisions on the river may have lasting, even permanent, consequences. On a river such as the Missouri, there's very little room for error. What makes it all the more complicated is that you won't be the most rational human being at 4 a.m. somewhere outside of Hermann. It was easier for us since there were four in our boat, the theory being that there would be a least one or two rational enough to determine if something we're about to do is unsafe.

For a solo paddler, consider what it's worth, then make sure you share that with your support crew. That way, if something happens along the route you won't be discussing it for the first time. Solo paddlers without a support crew have it the toughest. For you, there's no easy answer, but spend some time and think about safety attitude and how you plan on maintaining it over the course of the race.

So having just given a lecture on being safety aware and maintaining an attitude of "it's just a race" to minimize serious consequences, I need to come clean and admit I personally didn't follow my own advice. Here's what happened.

We were three hours outside of Hermann, 60 hours into the race. I was paddling along, feeling good and thinking about dinner in Hermann, when bam, my right hand goes numb.

As in N U M B. As in no feeling from my ring finger to my thumb. It didn't hurt. I still had enough strength to grip the paddle, but it was definitely numb.

So now what? We're three hours from the next checkpoint. I remembered thinking that it might be a stroke, but everything else felt okay, and my speech wasn't slurring, so I figured it wasn't that. But what was it? And more importantly, how threatening was it?

I analyzed every twinge and tweak as I continued to paddle. Three hours later when we pulled into Hermann there was no change, still numb. The good news was it wasn't worse; the bad news was it wasn't better. And I remember standing on the boat ramp, thinking, "What should I do?" The safest course of action would be to go to the Emergency Room and get it checked out. We were ahead of the clock enough that we could make a visit and still get back on the river in time. If not, there was always next year.

But then again, I'm still alive…

And I can almost see St. Charles 17 hours downstream…

So what the heck, let's go!

Eight months later as I write these words, my right hand is still numb[2]. It serves as a daily reminder of how we balance our decisions between safety and success. Would I have done it again? You bet. Would I have stopped if it got worse? Honestly I'm not sure I would have been that smart. Whatever your reaction to that event would be, develop your safety attitude and articulate it to your team. Before the race. And then realize that even when you have a safety game plan in place, it's not always clear what to do.

Team Safety

I was incredibly serious about the safety of my crew for one very simple reason: Those were my kids in the canoe, and that was my wife and Leigh driving the support van. It meant that, besides making sure I was fully prepared and keeping track of my own hydration, blisters, food intake and all those other details, I also needed to make sure I paid attention to everyone else's situation as well. It was my responsibility to continually balance the need to finish with the need to be smart to keep everyone safe.

I use the word "I" when really it's everyone's responsibility to watch out for everyone else. The tough part about coherency is that it's not necessarily obvious that you are or aren't. Oftentimes it's the case with tragic outdoor accidents that everyone assumes the leader's fine, because, well, he's the leader, when in reality he's not okay. Make sure all your team members are aware of their safety responsibility not only to themselves but to the rest of the team (which includes the Ground Crew). Make sure everyone is comfortable with expressing and discussing their concerns.

Safety of Other Race Participants

Oddly enough, the safety of other race participants, while just as important as the safety of your own team, is probably the hardest to address for two simple reasons. First, paddlers like us are totally focused on themselves and don't pay all that much attention to anyone else. While we should have been more aware of those around us, sadly we weren't. Secondly, we have enough of a challenge figuring out how coherent and safe we were, much less figuring out how somebody else was.

---

[2] After two nerve conduction tests and a high-resolution MRI, the doctors couldn't find the exact problem but surmised that the numbness was caused by lack of blood near a nerve due to all my paddling. Evidently nerves can grow back over time. The numbness has decreased some and I'm scheduled for another checkup to evaluate progress.

That paradox really hit home for us as we pulled into Washington around 4 a.m. Friday morning. Washington's not a checkpoint, but we were feeling very tired and besides, Washington has nice bathrooms.

As we pulled up to the boat ramp, there were already 10 or so MR340 paddlers just sitting on the ramp next to their boats. Although it was still dark, we could tell from their posture and general lack of response, they were absolutely exhausted (as were we).

Forty-five minutes later, after we had the chance to hit the bathrooms and take a quick nap on some picnic tables right next to the train tracks (by that time in the race you'll be able to sleep anytime, anywhere), many of those paddlers were still in the same position as when we arrived. As we loaded into the boat, I was mentally going over my own checklist starting with "Are we okay enough to continue?" I thought about the others still sitting on the ramp. Were they okay? Were they coherent enough to continue? Would they rest there long enough like us so they could make it the rest of the way? Is there anything we should do to help?

Then I realized as we pulled away that they were exactly where they should have been, on shore. It wasn't them that we should worry about; it was others that kept pressing onward in spite of their exhaustion that may have been in the most trouble.

On the river it gets even trickier to assess the safety of other participants. Sure, if there's someone standing in their kayak trying to bat at buoys with their paddle, it's a pretty good indication they're not all there. But for the most part what we saw were lots of very quiet focused paddlers making their way down stream. Were they coherent enough to be safe? Hard telling.

And while it wasn't necessarily up to us to judge the coherency of others, we were absolutely prepared to do anything and everything to help a fellow paddlers if they requested it, be it fishing them out of the water, sharing water or batteries, or just slowing down long enough to say "Hi" to see how they were doing and to talk about their trip so far.

If you see or talk to other paddlers where you have concerns, it's worth a quick cell phone call to the race directors. There's an incredible amount of safety boats and other race support along the route, and with the knowledge that a racer may need some help, they can get there in a hurry before something really bad happens.

Responsibility to the MR340

Finally, I bring up the safety of MR340 Race itself for a simple reason that without a keen focus on safety there wouldn't be a race.

People drown in the Missouri River every year. It's a tribute to Scott, his race staff and all the other safety groups helping that that type of tragedy hasn't occurred during the MR340. But while they contribute mightily keeping it safe, we as participants have a responsibility do our share. Not only for us today, but for the racers to come.

We need to prepare ourselves through awareness and approach. We need to make smart decisions and watch out for others.

We need to "Think Safety."

Letter of the Law

Our experience with the cruiser helps illustrate the difference between meeting the intent of being safe versus meeting the safety letter of the law. You can see this divide occur when people talk about something as simple as navigation lighting.

The question may be "Can I use glow sticks as navigation lighting?" Is that approach legally compliant to the rules? Sure. It's easy, they're cheap and emit the right color, so why not?

But take our encounter with Captain Ahab and add night to it with clouds covering up the moon and fog rising off the river. In that context the real question is this: Is our navigation lighting bright enough so that even Captain Ahab can see us so he doesn't run us over?

As with many things to do with safety, you'll see all kinds of people doing all kinds of things, with everyone happy until something bad happens. If we see you in Miami at 3 a.m. on Day 2 of the race and you say, "Hey Steve, we used MX Nuke Glow Sticks because they put out 80 lumens compared with 60 for typical sidelights," we're in sync. You did your homework. But if your answer is "We had to pick up something so we don't get disqualified and this was the only thing Walmart had…," remind yourself that Captain Ahab is still out there somewhere and that it's not about getting disqualified (DQ'd), it's about being safe.

Safety Approach

When I was a Boy Scout leader, I signed up to be certified in Red Cross First Aid. I fully expected going into the training that they would focus on the "How To's" like how to tie a bandage, how to tie a splint, how to do many different things to apply first aid. While they did address some of those topics, what surprised me was their overall approach. Everything they taught centered around two main concepts: First, keep the patient alive for approximately four minutes, and secondly, do no more harm to the victim while you're trying to keep him alive for four minutes.

What's so special about four minutes? Turns out that's the average length of time it takes for the cavalry (and the ambulance) to respond. Keeping a victim alive that long gives the pros enough time to get involved and do their part.

While that sort of training works great if medical assistance is that close by, it might not be all that helpful if you're canoeing or hiking deep in the wilderness. First aid training for those adventures centers on much longer term stabilization, since it may be days, not minutes, before help arrives.

For the MR340, while help is probably more than four minutes away, thankfully it's not days away. My personal estimation was we had to be ready to survive a catastrophe for 60 to 90 minutes while at the same time being able to signal our location. Based on this need, our safety approach consisted of being prepared by having the proper equipment and then having a response plan should something bad occur.

Don't look for trouble

Years ago, I took a Dale Carnegie public speaking class and vividly remember a talk from a man named Joe Gentile. Joe worked for UPS and his talk was on how to avoid accidents. He went into great detail about how UPS analyzed delivery accidents and found out a very high percentage of them were caused when drivers were backing up. The moral of his story: Don't back up.

I could see everyone's wheels turning. "Don't back up? What the heck is that?" But the older I've got, the more I've appreciated Joe's advice so I'll pass it along to you, but in this case it's "Don't look for trouble."

Not looking for trouble is more than just wearing a life vest and being ready to swim to shore. It's about making sure you are doing everything possible to avoid having to use the life vest in the first place (i.e. avoiding trouble). For us, we suspected trouble could come mainly from capsizing, bad weather, traveling at night and lack of alertness, so we did everything we could to avoid those situations.

Capsizing

We went to great lengths to avoid capsizing at all costs (almost to the point of paranoia) while at the same time making sure we were ready to recover if it happened. But being somewhat fatalistic, we realized that you could only do so much to avoid flipping, but with two lifeguards in the boat (Ellen and Christine), we felt our chances of making it to shore and getting cleaned up were pretty good. But we had a different view after talking with another tandem team about our close call with the cabin cruiser. Their attitude was "it's game over" if they swamped, and after considering what they said, we were a believer.

"It's not that we wouldn't be able to get to shore and get things back together," they said, "it's about the enormous amounts of energy we'd be spending gathering our stuff as it floats down in a 4-mph current, swimming to shore dragging a boat full of water." When you're cutting the finish line close to begin with, capsizing just isn't an option.

Our experience in capsizing came primarily from paddling lakes and Missouri streams. Normally, turning over in a canoe when you're in a stream requires you to not get between the canoe and a log, then wading a few feet to shore while dragging the canoe and collecting all your belongings while they're floating downstream. It's an inconvenience but usually not a show stopper.

Unfortunately, "wading ashore" and "Missouri River" aren't usually used in the same sentence.

For MR340 planning, we anticipated capsizing from the following:
• Impacting buoys, wing dikes, bridges and stationary sand dredges or barges
  • Waves from boats
  • Waves from wind
  • Getting run over by another boat or barge
  • Landing at a checkpoint
  • Paddling hard all on the same side
  • Flipping at the start from hitting/being hit by multiple boats combined with the river current (just see the 2009 Race DVD)

While this list may make it seem like the race is an endless dodge ball game, the reality is the race consists of hours upon hours of the same 3-4 mph current followed by a bridge followed by more hours of current followed by a checkpoint followed by more current...you get the picture. Understanding and anticipating what's slowly coming up goes a long way in preventing mishaps.

With that in mind, let's walk down the capsize list. You will have plenty of time to avoid both buoys and bridges since you'll be able to spot them quite a distance away. For buoys, it's about paying attention. While oddly spaced (I'm sure the Corps of Engineers has some sort of rationale), you'll see them much more frequently used on river bends than in straight sections. The key is to visually scan the river every so many paddles and mentally make note of where the buoys are and what side you'll pass them. Christine got into the habit of calling out "I see a buoy on the right" to make sure that Ellen in the stern saw it as well and was ready to adjust as necessary. It becomes even more important at night when you're depending on your flashlight. Take a break every 4-5 minutes to scan downstream and call out if you see a reflection from the buoy. Nighttime's also a good time to listen. You'll hear the rush of the water around the buoys (as well as the wing dikes), so when you stop to scan with the flashlight, listen as well.

Wing dikes by definition are not in the channel. Designed to direct the water away from the shore and into the channel, the easiest way to avoid wing dikes is to paddle in the middle of the channel. One of the common newbie mistakes is to think that cutting across the inside portion of a wide turn will be faster than following the channel on the outside portion of the bend. While it looks shorter, the current is much slower and you'll end up potentially scraping over submerged wing dikes (not to mention looking for trouble in the form of capsizing).

Bridges can be the most painful object you'll see on the river for the simple fact that you might be looking at it for hours before you finally pass underneath. Coming into Hermann Thursday night was especially agonizing for us since we literally looked at the Hermann bridge for two hours knowing that the next checkpoint (and dinner) was waiting just on the other side. Besides giving you plenty of warning, bridges also tell you where the channel is by marking what bridge span it's under with a green light (the other spans usually have red). Just aim for the green light and don't go too close to the bridge pylons. Bridge pylons create very intense hydraulics around them, and in some cases have large piles of driftwood stacked on the upstream side which may be hard to see at night.

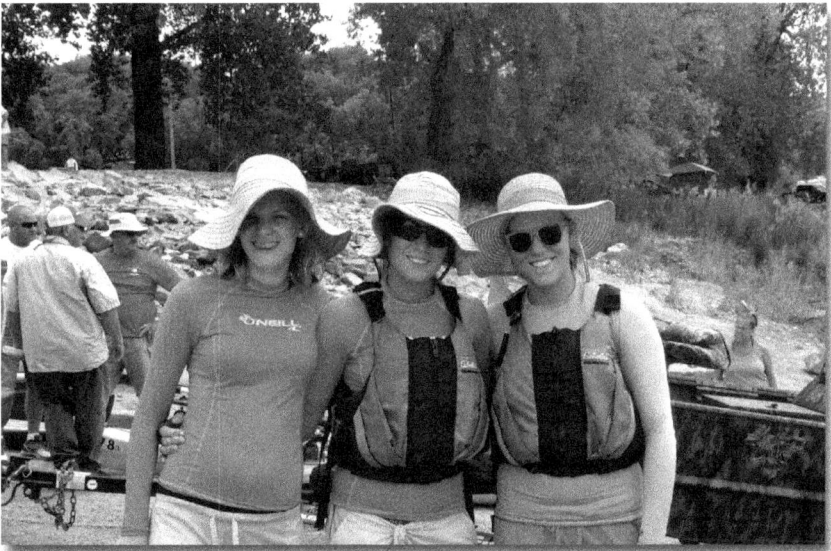

The girls at Glasgow getting ready to paddle. They're all smiles knowing that 82 miles from here is Jefferson City and a cool hotel room with a nice comfy bed. Notice the bass boat behind them. Boat ramps along the river are not reserved exclusively for MR340 racers, so we made sure we shared as much room as we could while on the ramp.

Moored barges and sand dredges gave me the most worry, mostly because I didn't bother to write down what mile marker they were at when they announced them at the safety meeting and kept second guessing myself every night. They are supposed to be illuminated at night, but there's no guarantee how visible they'll be and can be easy to miss in a lit up area near a city. As with bridge pylons, give them wide clearance since you don't want to risk hitting them and getting pulled under.

As you read earlier, boat wakes can be a real hazard. But we can tell you, in our 340 miles of paddling, that experience was our only encounter with capsize-threatening waves. The wake of a barge passing upstream two days later was tame compared to that boat. It's not that you won't see boats; it's just that most of them are either small enough that they don't generate much of a wake or that the bigger boats give you wide passage. That said, you need to be ready to paddle into the boat's wake at a 30- to 45-degree angle. This shallow angle allows you to roll up on the wave and slide down the other side. Letting waves hit you straight on the side of your boat is an easy way to roll over. Going into a wave at a 90-degree angle could cause your boat to be lifted by the waves at both the bow and the stern, with nothing but air underneath the middle and causing you to roll as well.

Barge traffic is kept to a minimum during the race. Barge operators are all aware that the MR340 is being held and take the proper precautions. If there are barges moving, you'll hear about them way in advance at the checkpoints since they move relatively slowly. Most barges don't throw off waves like a normal boat does but instead cause the water all around the barge to become agitated. Tows moving upriver generate larger, longer lasting waves. The more barges they're pushing, the larger the wake field will be. This "roughed up" water will bounce from shore to shore, so the water will stay choppy for a long time after the barge passes. If they mention barges at any of the checkpoints, ask what type of waves they're generating and how you should handle them.

Avoiding getting run over is all about assuming that the other boat can't see you and staying out of its way. When we saw a power boat coming toward us, we quickly moved to the outside of the channel (powerboats will usually stay in the channel), as far away as we could to keep out of their way and give them as much room as possible. In addition, we always made sure to point our bow into the wake as it approached to minimize rolling from side to side. Although we didn't see any power boats at night, our experience may have been an exception, so make sure your navigation lights are on and meet USCG range requirements.

Wind can be a real headache for paddlers and a potential cause of capsizing. White caps can form on the Missouri very easily within a short amount of time. Just as for boat wakes, try to head into the waves at a 30- to 45-degree angle (although you'll find this approach may aim you toward shore as opposed to downstream). Also consider if possible to add more weight to the front of the boat to keep the bow lower in the water. A higher bow is more susceptible to being blown around, making it hard to steer than a boat with the bow lower in the water (likewise, if the wind's blowing downstream, consider raising the bow since it can act as a sail). If it starts getting too rough, take cover close to shore. If it's still too rough, consider taking a shore break. If you think the water's rough when you're in the boat, imagine swimming around in white caps trying to collect things.

Besides causing you to capsize, the wind can also make matters much worse while you're swimming by blowing your now-empty boat upstream. That's where the throw rope comes in handy. If you exit unexpectedly, make sure you grab the boat first. Everything else can be recovered once you're back in the boat and using your spare paddle. Without the boat, there's not much you're going to do besides swim to shore and wait for help.

But for all the talk about the wind and the stories about being blown upstream, the Missouri River offers some real advantages over wind that you won't get on a typical large lake or bay. The river is relatively narrow in width and is protected with high banks and rows of trees to break the wind. While you'll absolutely encounter headwinds, there's usually very little side wind due to this protection.

We're also lucky that the Missouri River has an incredible amount of twists and turns, meaning that while the wind may be hammering you head-on for three miles straight, it might end up pushing you for the next three miles after you go around the bend.

The last big wind advantage the Missouri River has is, well, it's a river. If you get tired of paddling into the wind, just anchor your paddle in the water and let the river pull you along. It may be slow going for a few miles, but at some point the river's going to change direction.

Capsizing at the checkpoint or by all paddling on the same side are what we like to call a "whoops" capsize. That's where you're pulling up to shore and all get out on the same side at the same time and whoops, in you go. We made it a habit that Christine would be the first to get out, pull us closer up the boat ramp, then straddle the bow to stabilize it while everyone else jumped out, one at a time. It seems like such a silly procedure, but when you're tired and ready to jump out and grab some pizza from the Ground Crew, stupid things happen.

There was one other type of capsizing at checkpoints we need to mention. Most checkpoints are situated at boat ramps which are built to point slightly downstream (it keeps floating logs and debris off the ramp). Since there's more control paddling against the current than with it, our plan was for us to turn the boat around so it pointed up the river just upstream from the boat ramp, then paddle against the current onto the ramp. While this sounded good in theory, it was much easier to point the bow into the ramp, have Christine jump out and hold the bow, then let the current pivot the stern downstream so the boat's now pointing into the ramp. We had no trouble conducting this maneuver, thanks in part to the outstanding help provided by the volunteers manning the checkpoints. Be aware that the first set of checkpoints are very crowded, so you may end up spending a few minutes paddling in place waiting for boats to leave before you can dock.

Where the trouble comes in is if the checkpoint is close to a wing dike. The first time we encountered this at Jefferson City. The landing isn't a boat ramp but a sandy beach on the downstream side of a wing dike. As wing dikes push water into the channel, they create secondary currents that actually flow back upstream. Where paddlers get into trouble is when they cross over from the fast moving downstream current and enter into the current moving the other direction. While it usually isn't enough to flip the boat, it will absolutely spin your boat around. It's this surprise spin move that makes paddlers panic and flip themselves, when all they really had to do is paddle hard through the two currents and then straighten themselves out once they're fully behind the wing dike. The key to not having a problem is not being surprised when it happens.

Another "whoops" situation happens when all are paddling hard on the same side and someone almost goes in. We made sure we alternated sides when paddling to help us balance, and after a while it became second nature. Focusing on those habits early meant we were well practiced when Captain Ahab came flying up the river.

The last potential way we thought we could capsize was at the start. The 2009 MR340 Race video showed a couple of paddlers going in right as the gun went off, and I'm not sure they were even across the start line. Luckily, beginning the year we raced, they now have a staggered start, with the solo paddlers leaving at 7 a.m. and the teams leaving at 8 a.m. This approach greatly reduces the congestion and the opportunity for problems. You still have to worry about transitioning into the swift current of the Missouri from the slow moving Kaw River, but it wasn't nearly the problem we thought it would be.

We're sure there are other ways to go swimming, but this list is pretty inclusive on everything you'll encounter. Now that you know where it can occur, let's talk about what to do if it does happen.

One of our favorite family vacations was canoeing for a week in the Boundary Waters located in beautiful northern Minnesota. We paddled and portaged for two days before arriving at a quaint sandy cove where we set up camp. That accomplished, my kids did what they do best, entertained themselves in the great outdoors. For the next three hours, Linda and I sat on shore and watched our kids capsize, flip, swamp, spin, jump, sink, bail, push, tow, pull, and recover our canoes. Wildly entertaining and hilarious to watch, it didn't occur to me at the time that what my kids were really doing, besides having fun, was practicing MR340 recovery skills. That experience gave them the techniques and, more importantly, the confidence to react and recover should anything have happened during the race.

Just as we did, you too should consider finding a quiet lake to test and refine your swamping skills. Once there, get ready to get wet and find the answers to the following questions:

How stable is my boat? How far over do I have to lean to make it flip?

Will I fall out before it totally flips, or will it flip and then I fall out?

Are there parts of the boat or equipment I might get tangled in when it swamps?

Once swamped, will the boat right itself or will I need to help it rotate back over?

How well does my boat float when filled with water?

Is it possible to dump enough water out of the boat by rocking it side to side or is there another approach I might use to remove enough water so it's a least high enough where I can use a bailer or pump?

Is it better to stay outside the boat and tow it to shore, or is it better to roll back into the boat and paddle it submerged?

How does my life jacket feel when I'm in the water? Are there adjustments I need to make to make sure it doesn't ride up over my head?

Is it easier to float on my back? Can I dogpaddle when on my stomach?

No two swampings are the same. You will never be able to anticipate every potential situation, but getting experience in answering the above questions will at least give you a starting point. Should you still practice swamping even though you won't have access to your boat until the race? I recommend it strongly if you have any trepidation about swamping. Even if you practice using a different boat, you'll learn enough to still make it worthwhile.

One last comment about capsizing: As you paddle down the Missouri, make mental notes of what type of places are easier to land ashore. For example, sandbars are very easy to access since they usually have a gentle rise up from the river. Given the fact they may be close by, that's the first place I'd aim if swamped (although you may not see a sandbar for the first 70 miles). Another section that allows for easy access to shore is the outside bend of a turn. Usually there are no wing dikes to negotiate around, so it's very easy to get help from the current to push you toward shore. Your first reaction once capsizing may be to get to shore NOW, when in reality it might be simpler and safer to float along for awhile if somewhere downstream offers the opportunity for a much easier landing. The key is to recognize where those spots are and be constantly aware of where you are relative to them.

Night Traveling

We never practiced paddling on a river at night for two reasons: Comfort level and safety. We had been outside in full moons enough to realize what it was like, and because of that familiarity we didn't feel the need to risk practicing on the river at night with no safety boat or other support along for the ride. For us that turned out to be a good decision, but if you haven't been out at night in a full moon, or are uncomfortable with the thought about being out on the river at night, look around for full moon events. It's amazing how many hiking, biking and paddling events are held during a full moon. Keep an eye open for these types of events and join in if you get the chance. There's also lots of MR340 paddlers who will practice at night and let people know through the Forum. Most organizations will have all the safety considerations covered so all you'll have to do is show up and enjoy the fun.

For us, paddling at night was exactly what we thought it would be. Because we hadn't practiced, I was slightly anxious about night paddling when we started the race. But by the time we had cooked all day in the 104-degree heat, we were cheering for the sun to set and looking forward to paddling in the cool of the night.

Although not guaranteed, there was not one time during our three nights of paddling where we were out of sight of another boat. Certainly there were more boats on Tuesday night than on Thursday, but we were never alone on the river. In addition to other racers, every night we had at least one safety boat cruise up to say "hi" and see how we're doing. It's comforting to know that help is nearby just in case you need it.

We already talked about use of the flashlight and how to keep track of buoys and wing dikes. Besides seeing them, you'll also be able to hear them. Sound travels a long distance over water, so take a break from paddling every once in a while to listen for sound and direction of rushing water. We brought along a waterproof speaker so we could listen to music (more on that later) but always turned it off at sunset so we could hear rushing water (rushing water = bad day).

Staying in the channel is a little more problematic at night, since it's harder to see channel markers on the shore. But by the time you get to Tuesday night, you'll already have had 14 hours of practice, and by then you'll be a seasoned pro at staying in the middle of the channel. One option which our friend Mike Claypool and his team used was to have their GPS loaded with a "trail" of the channel (look on the Rivermiles Forum). All they had to do is stay on the path indicated by their GPS.

One challenge with nighttime paddling is foreshortening, where the distance to shore looks closer than it is due to shoreline being hidden by shadows and moon reflections off the trees along the bank. This effect seems to reverse as you get closer to the shore where it seems to sneak up on you.

Another safety suggestion when traveling at night is to watch when people are leaving checkpoints. Which direction the river is going around a bend can be somewhat confusing at night. At times, the river can appear to be a big lake that goes nowhere. We found that having a boat in front of you at a distance provided enough directional cues to understand what course the river's taking. Because of that, I always tried to time our leaving with somebody else's. You don't necessarily have to leave the exact instant they do, but having somebody in front a half of mile or so (five minutes ahead at a 6 mph pace) is a great way for someone to help guide you down the river.

Weather

During my Boy Scout trip with my son to Philmont, our crew had an overnight stop at Head of Dean Camp near Mount Baldy. Located high up on the head of a huge, open valley, the camp office had a covered porch where we could sit and look for miles down the valley where we had just hiked. We were there relaxing mid-afternoon when BOOM, here came rain. And rain it did, with bucketfuls of water pouring down from the sky. As we sat, dry and comfortable looking out over the valley, we noticed a small orange blob coming up the trail far below. As it continued to pour, more blobs of color appeared. We soon realized that it was another group of Scouts, hiking up the valley from where we had been earlier that day. Torrents of water were rushing down the trail where they were hiking. Lightning crackled in the sky, and the wind whipped all around. We watched in silence, thinking to ourselves how miserable they must be hiking in that kind of storm.

They were only 50 yards away from the cabin when, like someone shutting off a spigot, the rain stopped and the sun peeked out from the clouds. As they clomped onto the porch, thoroughly drenched and dispirited, I thought in hindsight that all they had had to do was hunker down 20 minutes for the rain to blow over and they could have hiked up the valley in the sunshine under one of the biggest rainbows we ever saw.

Maybe our Scout friends didn't know most afternoon rainstorms in that part of Philmont hit quick but blow over just as fast. Maybe they didn't know how dangerous it was to hike in an open field during a lightning storm. Or maybe they knew but were convinced they needed to make camp before a certain time. Whatever they thought, the result was they ended up slogging through something they could have just as easily avoided.

Where they failed is where you need to succeed. There may be times during the race when it's safer to wait out the storm, or the fog, or the heat, rather than keep going. There are other times where keeping going is the best option to avoid bad weather behind you. Your mission is to understand the weather forecast and use it to plan, and replan, accordingly.

The temperament of the Missouri River is very consistent over the course of the race. What you'll see of the river on Tuesday morning at Kaw Point will be very similar to what you'll see 340 miles later.

Not so with weather. Not only can the weather change dramatically over a very short period of time, it can also evolve as you paddle all the way across the state. Thankfully weather forecasting has come a long way since the days of Lewis and Clark. With apps such as Weather.com and myRadar, both you and your Ground Crew will have up-to-the-minute weather status and predictions.

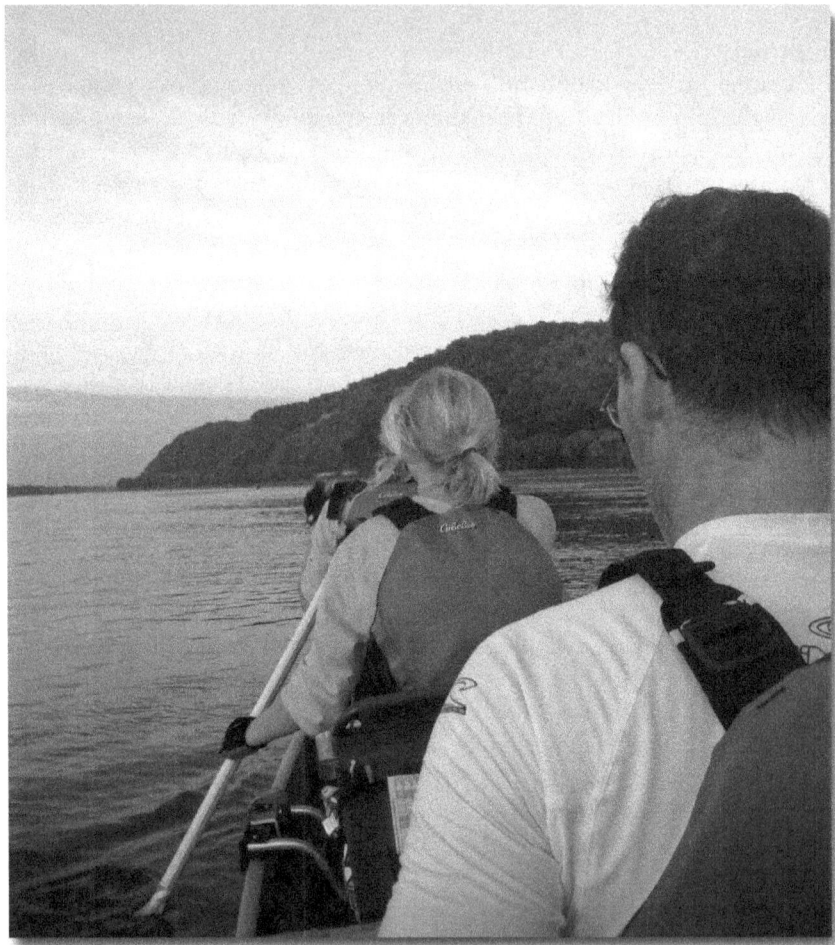

A beautifully calm and serene Missouri River as we headed into Hermann on Thursday night. Dusk, evening and early morning was very quiet on the water, but the wind would kick up by mid-morning as the sun started to heat things up.

Based on that regularly consulted weather forecast, here are some questions you should ask:

1) Do I have the correct gear for the forecasted weather condition? (Remember you're only trying to carry only the gear you need to get you to the next checkpoint.)

2) What potential safety issues should I be watching for as a result of this weather condition?

3) How will my remaining time on the clock affect my decision to stop or continue?

Out of all those decisions, remaining time on the clock is the one that will get you in the most trouble. Although your go/no go decision based on weather conditions should be the same no matter how much time is left, the reality is as you get closer and closer to the DQ time, the more you'll be willing to take chances you normally wouldn't take. The easiest solution, as Joe Gentile would say, is to not look for clock trouble in the first place. If the forecast is calling for potential weather problems, adjust your race strategy to build up time on the clock so you're not forced to make a decision between being DQ'd or paddling in an unsafe weather condition.

What type of weather will you encounter during the summer in Missouri? Here's a short list:

Rain – Summer rain in Missouri typically comes in three forms. The first, and potentially the most dangerous, is the multi-cell rainstorm, or squall line. Formed at the boundary line of hot and cold air, these types of storms pack lots of energy. They may consist of heavy rain, hail, lightning, high winds and tornados. The good part about these storms is that forecasters usually can predict when and where the line will hit. While local variations in intensity occur, in many cases you'll know within a few hours when it will arrive, how violent it will be, and how long it will take to pass through. Ideally you'll be near cover at a checkpoint, but if you're caught out on the river, pulling onto the shore on the side where the storms are coming from will allow the bank to give you some protection from the wind and driving rain.

The second type of rain is the single-cell storm. These storms emerge in the afternoon and, like our experience at Philmont, are localized events that pass through very quickly. Oftentimes they'll be rain and lightning in one area, and the sun will be shining five miles away. Just as you would when caught in a squall line, you'll want to be off the river if a single-cell storm hits, but the good news is it will pass fairly quickly.

The last type of rain is the perfect type for paddling: Cool rain showers. As long as there's no lightning and the winds are reasonable, paddling through this won't be a problem (although you'll have to keep up with the bailing).

Lightning – We were very watchful of lightning. There's no cover on the river itself, so if you're in the middle, you're the highest point. If we saw lightning or heard thunder, our plan was to move as close to shore as possible, where the trees nearby could take the brunt of the storm. If it got too bad we would have pulled the canoe out of the water, turned it over, and taken shelter underneath. What's "too bad?" That's hard to say, but if you see lightning or hear thunder, right then is a good time to get close to shore and not be a target.

Fog – Unlike with rain, most of us have very little wilderness experience with fog. Where we might encounter fog just once every few years where we live, fog on the river is a common occurrence, and chances are you'll encounter some form of it multiple times during the race.

Fog develops when a combination of weather events happen concurrently: A cloudless night where the surface cools by radiating heat to the atmosphere, light wind, relative humidity near 100%, and the air temperature and dew point within 4-5 degrees Fahrenheit. When these events occur, the water vapor in the air will condense to form water droplets. Depending on the density of these droplets, the result may be classified as mist, when there's visibility of greater than 0.6 miles (1 km), or fog, when visibility is less than 0.6 miles. Fog will be thickest closer to the water (where the paddlers are) and thin out the higher it is away from the water source. How dense it will be and how deep it gets depends on the intensity of the combined weather events.

On the river, fog raises a number of safety issues primarily due to poor visibility and reduced sound. Think of our earlier discussion on navigation lighting. USCG regulations stated the sternlight was to be visible two miles away. By the time vapor is classified as fog, visibility is down to one-third of that distance. What's worse, not only is your visibility limited in seeing bridges, barges, buoys, boats and wing dikes, so is the visibility of other boats seeing you, especially since your navigation lights may be of little help. One point that made a lasting impression on us was a picture shown at the Monday night safety meeting. The bottom part of the photo just shows fog, but the top shows the pilot house of a tow boat. When you first look at it, the picture almost looks like two images were pasted together, but after you look for a few more seconds, you realize that it's one picture since fog by definition will be close to the water. The message was clear: The barge pilot may be in sunshine, whereas paddlers like us can be buried and un-noticed in the fog.

Being in fog can also be very disorientating since all your normal visual reference points may be hidden. One paddler on the Rivermiles Forum talked about how they were paddling in fog, feeling like they were making good time. But when the fog started burning off, they realized they were paddling upstream. Seems hard to imagine that someone wouldn't know the difference between upstream and downstream on something that has a 4-mph current, but it does give a good illustration about how confusing it can get when there's no visual point of reference.

Fog usually appears from very early in the morning (3 a.m.) through daybreak, and starts to "burn off" from the top down as the sun rises. Depending on density and depth, it may take until mid-morning to clear.

I find myself using the word "depending on" quite often in this section, but that's the nature of fog. There's so many weather variables involved, not to mention contributions from things like power plants, tributary inputs with colder water and terrain, that it's very difficult to project exactly when and where fog will occur.

Transmission of sound, or lack of it, is another safety concern. Because sound is attenuated by the fog, normal sounds like rushing water over wing dikes or around buoys will be muted, so you will not have the reaction time as you would on a clear day or night. Also, sound may not be directional; it may seem to be coming from directions other than its real source.

Be aware that fog not only presents a challenge for the paddler but for safety boats as well. The safety boat's lack of visibility and muted, non-directional sound is a big hindrance in trying to rescue someone, all while the safety boat tries to avoid the same boats, barges, buoys, wing dikes, etc., so it doesn't turn from a rescuer to a rescuee. For those reasons, safety boats are instructed to pull off the river during thick fog. All the more reason for you to pull over as well.

So what's the best way to address fog?

First and foremost, be ahead of the clock enough where you can afford a 3-5 hour weather delay. Don't be driven to do unsafe things like go into a thick fog bank just because you'll DQ if you don't. You may start to feel like you've got lots of time if you're three hours ahead going into Jefferson City, but be aware that a time cushion can quickly vanish if you're stuck on shore, waiting for the fog to lift.

Secondly, talk to the checkpoint officials. There are safety boats all along the course and will provide up-to-date weather reports that get passed along to each of the checkpoints. Ask the officials: What are they hearing from the safety boats? How long will it last? What do they recommend?

Finally, if life gives you lemons, make lemonade. If fog's going to make travel unsafe for a few hours, be ready to spend that time wisely by getting some sleep. You might have to adjust your downstream plans, but that's where adaptability comes into play. Make the most of your downtime by getting rest.

Heat – For paddlers like me who usually drive a desk in a comfortable, air-conditioned building, baking in 104-degree heat for four days is a real concern. Unlike cold, where you can add more layers, surviving and competing in heat takes a combination of many different approaches.

Minimize sun exposure - We minimized our exposure to the sun through the use of light-colored, breathable long-sleeve shirts and pants; light because light clothes reflect the sun better (the more the sun reflects, the cooler you are), and breathable so sweat evaporates better, cooling you down. I know there are many who disagree with me by saying, "I spend all summer in a t-shirt and shorts so I can manage it for this race." They may, of course, be right (especially if they're a roofer), but then again, they may be wrong. The problem comes when you find out too late that it isn't a good approach. If you're unsure, you can always bring both (clothing is light weight and small in packing size) and switch back and forth.

Each of us had a straw gardener's hat. You'll be getting sun from all around and reflections off the water because of the twists and turns of the river. Our straw hats did a good job protecting us from sun all the way around. They were also very inexpensive just in case we lost one.

Keep hydrated – We'll spend a whole section on hydration, but for now, remember that drinking enough cool fluids helps lower your temperature.

Eat cold – Besides drinks, there's lots of cold food you can use to lower your temperature. We brought grapes that we kept in a cooler, but the folks in the Miami checkpoint did us one better by freezing cantaloupe and grapes. They sure tasted good and cooled you down as well.

Misters or wet towels – We brought both along with us. Soak towels in your cooler, then wrap them around your head or drape over your neck. We used misters to spray ourselves in the face and arms.

Ice – Ice was my "Plan B" to use when nothing else was working. I brought along two 10-pound bags of ice at the start of the race, one to keep the food cold, the other to keep us cool. While we paid a tremendous weight penalty, having instant access to ice meant we could react much sooner to any heat-related issues.

Pace – How is pace related to heat? Pushing too hard when it's hot is a sure way to get into heat-related problems. Our approach was not to over-exert ourselves during the heat of the day. The cool of the evening or the dark of night is the perfect time to put the hammer down. Take it easier in the heat of the day.

Sleep – There's no law that says you have to sleep at night. If given a choice, plan your sleep for the heat of the day. Late morning on Wednesday and Thursday found us sleeping, not paddling in the heat.

Asian Carp – You won't find any reference to them in Lewis and Clark's journals, because Asian carp is a fairly new addition to the Missouri River ecology, having been introduced into the Mississippi River and then into the Missouri from fishponds during the flood of 1993. Not from around here and having no competition or predators to stabilize their numbers, the Asian carp has literally taken over many parts of rivers, especially the Illinois River as it winds its way up to Chicago.

While it's bad enough that they've upset the river ecosystem, they also are a danger to boaters and paddlers. If a school of these fish get excited or agitated, they will literally jump two to three feet out of the water. If they were small, that might not be so bad, but these fish can weigh 20 pounds or more. If you're in a moving boat, getting hit by a 20-pound object isn't pleasant and could cause injury as well as knock you out of the boat. Asian

Carp do not like fast moving water. They are usually found in the slower water between wing dikes or directly adjacent to shore.

I have been on the Missouri River many times and have never seen them jump, but I do know people who have been right in the middle of them. They're out there, but it's not like they advertise their whereabouts. Our approach to these carp was very simple: Duck until they stop jumping. Trying to paddle away means you're more exposed to getting hit. Duck and relax until they stop.

Alertness

Because it's a 2,341-mile river that drains more than half a million square miles, the Missouri River is a place where you'll need to keep alert. For us it was much easier than most teams since with four paddlers we only needed one or two attentive at any given time, but if you're on a tandem team or going solo, it's critical that you stay alert and, more importantly, understand when you're not alert so you can pull over. There's no one simple thing you'll do to be sure you're alert. Certainly things like caffeine, music, conversation and taking breaks all help. But in the end it comes down to paying attention to how alert you are, then having the discipline to take a break when you need to, so something bad doesn't happen.

The challenge, then, is to recognize when you're not alert. Unfortunately that's not very easy to do. Take a look at Christine's MR340 YouTube video of our race (http://youtu.be/Y3TEn5hIw-Q). It's interesting to see how our alertness ebbed and flowed over four days. I was convinced prior to looking at the video that we were always alert enough to continue the race. After looking at the video, I'm not so sure.

What do you do when you find your alertness ebbing? Take a quick break. For us it was easy. Whoever wanted to take a break let everyone else know that they were going to take a quick nap, then they slept while the others paddled. If you're a solo paddler, it's a little tougher, you'll have to pull along the shore for your break. You don't even have to get out of your boat, you just want to be at a calm spot where you won't unknowingly float away.

But taking a break doesn't mean a two hour time penalty. We found closing our eyes for 15 minutes or so did wonders for our alertness. These sorts of breaks won't replace your need for longer term sleep, but they will rejuvenate you enough to keep going in a safe manner.

Safety Summary

To summarize what we discussed in our section on safety, safety is more than about you; it is critical for your team, your Ground Crew and all those other paddlers in the race. Safety's not just following the letter of the law. It is understanding why the rules are there and making sure you're compliant to their intent. Avoid safety issues in the first place by doing the right thing at the right time and by not looking for trouble. Finally, have a plan to execute if something happens, and make sure your team and your Ground Crew know your plan.

PART III

ENDURE

PART III - ENDURE

To finish, you'll need to endure 340 miles of river. Based on our experience and what we saw, we divided issues concerning endurance into two major categories:

1. *"This wasn't what I thought it was going to be..."* - Occurring early in the race, this category is comprised of individuals and teams who, from a preparedness standpoint, may have not recognized what they were really getting into.

2. *"This sucks?"* - Caused by a multitude of discomforts building up over time to a point where they've said, "That's it, I'm done."

"Hey! How's it going?" I yelled across the creek. On a sunny, late winter Sunday I took Claire and her two friends on a hike in Meramec State Park. As the girls and I were taking a break on a small sandbar, we spotted five hikers on the other side, so I gave them a shout just to see how they were doing. Turns out they were members of the St. Louis Adventure Club, and they, like us, decided to take advantage of the beautiful day to get in some hiking. Before we knew it, we were tagging along with them to visit Green Cave, located high up on a cliff overlooking the Meramec River. As we talked and I learned about their group's other hikes and adventures, I got to thinking about the MR340 and how my new friends would fair on that adventure.

One-third of the paddlers that did not finish on our MR340 stopped paddling by Waverly, the second checkpoint, which is 73 miles, or one-fifth of the way, into the race. This number of DNFs for these first two checkpoints is probably on the low side since there were a few cases where one paddler stopped and the remaining team, even if only one was left, kept paddling. I suspect that if asked what went wrong, many of those paddlers who ended the race at that point would have responded, "This isn't what I thought it would be…" The first part to enduring this race is the ability to change this response around to one of two different replies: "This race is what I thought it would be" or "This isn't quite what I thought it would be, but how cool is this?"

My family is hard core. From canoeing in the Boundary Waters to hiking up the tallest mountain in Colorado, my family has been on some pretty challenging vacations over the years. It wasn't that big of a stretch for us to add a 340-mile adventure to our resumes. As a parent, I should have been concerned whether or not they'd be able to survive 340 miles worth of paddling, but having seen them in action on a mountain, on a lake, in massive rainstorms, I knew they could handle it because they had handled similar challenges in the past. But the phrase "it isn't what I thought it would be" got me thinking about our prior adventures. Hiking up the tallest mountain in Colorado certainly wasn't like anything we thought it would be, but we made it anyway. Paddling in wilderness two days away from anything wasn't quite what we thought it would be either, but we made it and had a great time doing it. That's when it struck me. Our success on the MR340 wasn't because we hiked or biked or paddled before, it was because we knew that our adventures were never quite like we imagined, yet we still kept coming back for more. It was our understanding of what adventure really was that made the next adventure possible. How cool it that?

It's one thing to spend your whole life with someone like your own child to understand what's they're capable of; it's another thing to pick a paddling partner you may or may not know very well. Think back to my St. Louis Adventure Club friends. Would I go with any one of them, even though I only met them for a few hours? You bet. Why? Because their love and attitude for adventures would translate perfectly into the MR340 adventure.

"But wait a minute," you might be thinking. "Granted, your friends have adventure experience, but wouldn't you rather pick an athlete, someone who's a half-marathon runner or a biker? After all, the MR340 is an endurance event." While I understand the reasoning (MR340 = Endurance = Athlete), there are two important distinctions between an adventurer and an athlete that makes the adventurer more desirable for this race: Duration and variability. Think of how a half-marathoner trains. Their practice sessions focus on different facets of their event. Training components like pace, strength, posture, endurance and decision making are all geared around maximizing their ability to physically get from Point A to Point B. In most half-marathon training programs, runners will culminate in a 12-mile run two weeks before, meaning that they will have not experienced the last 1.1 miles of the race. When the actual race is run, the only variables the runner may not have encountered besides the last mile is the course steepness profile and the weather.

Now compare that to the MR340. In the time the half-marathoner takes to drive to the race, run the race, cool down, drive home and soak in the tub, you won't even have made it to the first checkpoint. It's that duration that drives the number of variables you'll encounter. Sleep, weather changes and nighttime paddling are all variables to be wrestled with and are driven by the length of time you're out on the river. Your training can be designed to address some of these areas, but it's difficult to get the full effect without actually doing something that long in duration.

Consider the half-marathoner's longest training run for a moment. The equivalent length for the MR340 would be approximately 311 miles. I don't know about you, but there was no way we were going to fit in that kind of practice prior to the race. What we counted on instead was our ability to handle adventure.

All this is not to say that athleticism isn't important or helpful. It just helps illustrate that the athlete part of the MR340 is but a small component of the overall race for a first timer. Would I give the same advice to West Hansen, a world-class paddler and multiple winner of the MR340 men's solo division? No way. By the time you get his level of experience, athleticism plays a much larger role in his ability to finish with a sub-40 hour time. The key distinction between you as a first timer and West is that you still have some learning to do.

Is it possible to not have all that prior adventure experience and still finish? Sure, but here's where preparation helps. First, if you have a choice, pick a partner that fits the St. Louis Adventure Club mold. Your partner doesn't have to be a hard-core paddler; they just need to be hard-core adventurer (paddling they can learn). If you're worried that you or your paddling partner is still light on adventure, try one of the shorter river paddling events like the Kawnivore 100 (www.rivermiles.com/kawnivore-100/) or Race to the Dome (www.racetothedome.org/). They're not 340 miles but are long enough to let you know if the MR340 is the race you thought it will be. Finally, remember the key word is "adventure" and not necessarily "paddling." Even if you can't make these shorter length paddling events, look instead for other adventures like hiking, biking and running. While not necessarily directly applicable to the MR340, what you're really doing is learning about adventure and, more importantly, how to handle it.

"This Sucks" – Understanding Discomfort Management

My understanding of discomfort management started when I became an adult leader in my son's Boy Scout troop. While I'm sure I encountered it when I was a Scout, it was only when I was an adult that I truly understood the concept.

We'd go on a campout and, sure enough, it would rain. (How do you know Troop 613 is camping? It's raining out.) That gave our troop lots of opportunity to practice with rain gear. As a leader watching the kids, it was a pretty basic scenario. If it rained and they forgot their rain gear, it was going to suck. If it rained and they brought their rain gear, it was going to be a pretty fun time. For us as leaders, it was our job to let the kids experience a degree of discomfort as part of the learning process but not to the point of them quitting or it becoming a safety issue.

Some Scouts never had to learn that particular lesson. They had already figured out that rain gear was an important part of being prepared. Some had to learn the rain gear lesson one or two times before they figured it out, and a few never learned at all. But these encounters helped remind me that while we can't control the rain, we can absolutely manage our discomfort with some very simple planning. For you on the MR340, there's no Scoutmaster watching out for you. You'll have to be your own discomfort manager.

Discomfort Management

The need to manage discomfort became even clearer once I started training for a marathon. The first mile or two of my training runs would be unbelievably horrible, then I'd settle down into a fairly consistent, tolerable pace for the remainder of the run. I kept wondering how in the world I was going to make it 26 miles when the first two sucked that badly. Then I had the chance to talk with Ben Rosario, former owner of Big River Running here in St. Louis. He competed in the U.S. Olympic Trials, and it was almost uncanny how he described the initial discomfort he had to go through when running a race. That helped me to realize that what he was good at (besides running) was managing his discomfort. It wasn't that he didn't encounter discomfort (he did all the time). He knew ways to work around it to keep it at a tolerable level. His shoes, socks, food intake, hydration and mental preparation prior to the race maximized his level of performance while minimizing, but not eliminating, his level of discomfort.

For the MR340, your mission is to manage your discomfort in order to make it to Jefferson City. Exceed your discomfort threshold and you'll quit. Manage it to a reasonable level and you'll make it. Think about the statistics for a moment. Why is Jefferson City the magical place that drastically reduces DNFs? Because by the time you get there you'll have either figured out how to manage discomfort, or you'll have quit. It's just that simple.

One important thing to understand about how high-performance athletes fight discomfort is knowing that they spent countless hours of training and racing, all the time experimenting and understanding how close they can get to the edge without going over. You probably won't have that same luxury of training, meaning you'll need to keep a higher margin between your current race discomfort level and your potential "quit line." Just as everyone's quit line is at a different level, so is everyone's ability to recover if they accidently go close to or over it.

Also be aware that your quit line changes over the course of the race. Rain at Katfish Katy's (Mile 180) will have a different discomfort impact two days into the race compared with rain occurring at the start.

Be Happy

Some more effervescent readers will point out that life doesn't suck and that you really should think positive. For those, we suggest you use a Happy Meter as opposed to a discomfort ranking. Whether the glass is half full or half empty, what you're really trying to do is to stay away from the quit line.

I'm a glass half-full type of person, and thinking about discomfort from the happy side opens your mind to lots of fun ways for cheap and easy happiness during the race which goes a long way in relieving discomfort and acts as an accumulated advantage. As an example, one of my favorite drinks is a 32 oz. Diet Coke from a fountain. So what did the Ground Crew get me as we got ready to leave Glasgow? One frosty cold Diet Coke from Casey's General Store in downtown Glasgow, and suddenly I'm a new person.

In the next sections we'll talk about drinking, eating and what equipment works best, but as you read, think about what would make you happy. That Diet Coke made me happy but at the same time was part of my hydration strategy. It's okay to use happiness with race strategy to accumulate advantages.

In addition, don't be stingy. I overheard one paddler talking about how they didn't eat their candy bar until they hit Hermann (had to be sometime on Day 3). I ate my peanut butter cookies halfway to Lexington, four hours into the race. While I'm sure that was part of the paddler's motivational approach to wait that long, there's nothing wrong with experiencing happiness earlier and more frequently if that's what it takes to better manage your discomfort.

Hydration

Discomfort management starts with proper hydration. It's the foundation for all your other activities needed to complete the race. Become dehydrated and you run a greater risk of headaches, nausea, dizziness, loss of appetite and fatigue, all sure-fire contributors to increase the probability of quitting.

The solution should be easy. Just drink enough liquids. But your ability to drink the right amount of liquids is controlled by availability and accessibility.

At the awards banquet, one solo paddler talked about running out of drinking water midway between checkpoints, and how racers around her quickly offered theirs. While her story is a great illustration of just how generous MR340 racers are, the only thing I could think about was just how close to a bad day she was about to have by running out of water and being 3-4 hours away from the next stop. If you run out of liquids, you'll hit your quit line pretty fast. The lesson we took away from her story was that even for experienced paddlers, it's extremely hard to accurately project hydration needs over a long period.

Our solution? Carry an overabundance of liquid for each paddler.

"But wait," you say, "you just gave the lecture about weight, and now you say oversupply on liquids?"

You bet. Out of all the things that can make you quit, dehydration will cause it sooner than the extra poundage more liquid brings (approximately 8.3 pounds per gallon of water). What you're really doing by bringing more liquids than you potentially think you need is buying a discomfort prevention insurance policy.

Taken at the end of the race, this picture illustrates all the equipment we brought onboard including the water jug and hose hydration system and the mounting of the GPS. Tightly secured for probably two-thirds of the race, the equipment began to get very sloppily stowed towards the end.

So what combination of liquids should you bring? In our case it was half water and half something else (preferably something that provides happiness). The half and half part came from our running experiences. In road races it is recommended that you alternate between water and sports drinks at each water stop, the theory being that sports drinks alone are hard on the kidneys since your body may need to filter out unused sugar and nutritional supplements, and water alone isn't enough to resupply electrolytes.

But proper hydration is more than having adequate liquids onboard; it's also about making sure you're drinking what you brought. And while it sounds strange, we've found that accessibility is just as important as availability.

There are a number of different approaches to keeping liquids available. Probably the simplest one is having a large cooler that contains individually bottled water and sports drink for the whole boat crew. The advantage is that everything that needs to be cold is located together and resupply is a snap, just dump in some drinks with ice and you're off. Another variation is to provide smaller coolers for each member of the crew. Here the advantage is the cooler is closer to the paddlers, and it's also much easier for the Ground Crew to check on each paddler's individual liquid consumption.

Another accessibility method is the use of hydration systems. Similar to Camelbak hydration systems for daypacks, this method uses a tube and mouthpiece connected to a container full of liquid. The difference from a traditional Camelbak is the tube may be connected to a water jug instead of a bladder. We've seen setups where crews will use these tubes to tap off one large jug, or each crewmember may have his own. Something to remember when using tubing is that on a hot day the liquid tends to get warm. The farther away the source, the more hot water you're going to drink (or spit out).

In our experience hiking and backpacking, people who used hydration tube systems never had a problem with dehydration. Conversely, people who kept their Nalgenes buried in a pocket of their backpack and who had to ask someone to get it for them were much more likely to have problems. The difference? Ready accessibility. With a hydration tube, since it's right there, you tend to take smaller drinks but more often. When liquids aren't accessible, there's more effort involved not only for yourself but for whoever's closer to the cooler. The result is you may be putting off hydrating longer than you should, with potentially bad results. That said, any of the methods above will work; just be aware that the farther away the liquid, the more conscious effort you'll need to make to keep hydrated.

For our race, we went with a combination of individual coolers and hydration tubes. Each cooler could hold approximately three 32-ounce Gatorades and two to three 16-ounce water bottles. We attached the hydration tubes' mouthpieces to our lifejackets and connected them to a gallon water jug we put underneath the seat.

Our approach was to keep a substantial part of the water separate and then bring bottled water, soda and Gatorade. The bottled water makes it convenient to mix powdered teas and drink flavors. These mixes weigh next to nothing but provide a great change of pace. We avoided mixing anything with our main water source since once the flavor goes in, it's very hard to get the taste out.

A word of caution about liquids: Make sure you've sampled each beverage you're bringing to make sure it doesn't cause problems (this goes with food as well). I never had a problem with any Gatorade products until I drank Xtremo Tropical Intenso (What the hell is that???) on a training run. Puking or having the runs on dry land is bad enough, but it's horrific on the water. Avoid the problem by sampling flavors or brands (and all food choices) ahead of time.

For most of us, caffeine plays a large role in our daily lives. If you're looking to get a massive headache, avoid drinking anything caffeinated. If you're a caffeine addict like us and are trying to minimize withdrawal during the race, you'll need to make sure you have ample supply of caffeine. Excedrin Migraine, Energy Beans and No Doz help keep up the caffeine level, but for us we did the simple thing and carried soda and Starbuck's Iced Coffee. Besides having caffeine it was a nice change of pace from water and Gatorade.

But wait a minute. Starbucks? On the world's longest non-stop canoe and kayak race? It's a grueling 80+ hour athletic event, you say, not some sort of picnic!

While you're right about the grueling part, the reality is it's much different athletically than running/biking/swimming events. On this race, your heart rate will probably never hit your 80% threshold line (barring Captain Ahab), so the whole concept of downing drinks that provide 30 minutes worth of kick aren't near as relevant as a wide variety of foods and liquids that keep you consistent and happy. This race is about pushing yourself to move forward but at a very constant and sustainable pace. Picking a wide array of food and drinks will help better than a pure racing diet.

Our initial liquid resupply concept was for each paddler to pull out their individual cooler and water jug and hand them to the Ground Crew, but it turned out it was just as easy having the Ground Crew refill every container while they were in the canoe using a 10-pound bag of ice and a 5-gallon water jug carried from the car. The key to this approach was our ability to land our canoe in a place that was easily accessible to the Ground Crew.

The down side of having a majority of your liquids hidden in a jug is that it's next to impossible to know how much you've drank, much less knowing how your other crew members are faring. But for us, the use of hydration tubes enabled us to not have any hydration problems.

Which leads to the next discussion…how do you know when you're correctly hydrated?

Nature Calls

Having to urinate is a sure sign of good hydration, but it's awfully inconvenient when you're in a boat. It's a balancing act for this race to drink enough to be hydrated while at the same time not drinking too much so you have to go every 15 minutes.

There is such a thing as over hydration. Referred to as water intoxication or hyponatremia, it occurs when huge amounts of fluids are consumed, causing disruptions in the body's normal electrolyte levels. Although rare, it can be potentially fatal. Even though it's a potential concern, you're much more likely to encounter dehydration issues as opposed to over hydration. To prevent either, keep close watch of how much liquids you consume by tracking both how much you drink and how much you urinate and compare that with what's your normal frequency.

But what's normal? Let me ask a personal question. How often do you urinate in a typical day? If you're like me you probably don't think about how often you go because it's usually not a big deal, there's bathrooms all around. But knowing your frequency of bathroom stops provides two pieces of useful information for the race. First, from a planning standpoint it lets you think about how often you'll be stopping to go. Secondly, your frequency of urination serves as a benchmark during the race to determine if you're maintaining your hydration. For example, I usually urinate seven to 10 times during the course of a normal day, so if I'm in the canoe for seven hours and hadn't pottied, that's a good indication I'm not drinking enough.

But this is a race and nothing close to a normal day, so wouldn't you expect your urination pattern to be different? Ideally there won't be that much of a change since as we've talked about before, you're thinking about maintaining yourself over days, not hours. Is it okay that you urinate only twice in a period as opposed to a more normal four times. Sure, but it's not okay to not go at all.

So what's the best way to go? In answering that question let me respond in two ways, theoretically and in reality. In theory, since we're all stewards of the river, we would do our utmost not to spoil the river with our effluence. Therefore we would approach our bathroom breaks in one of the prescribed manners. If we pottied in the boat, we'd go in a sealable container that would then be disposed of at a checkpoint bathroom. If we decided to go on shore, we would select a spot 100 feet from the water in which to do our business.

Now let's talk reality. We considered a number of different ways to go to the bathroom. In keeping with our strategy of staying in the boat as much as we could, we urinated in our plastic bailer (a windshield wiper fluid jug with the bottom cut off). For guys this is pretty easy to do. For ladies this is slightly more challenging, so we ended up buying each of the girls a Go Girl female urination device (www.go-girl.com, $13 each). Advertised as a way for a woman to "take life standing up" (or in our case, kneeling down in a crowded canoe), it was just the ticket for the girls to relieve themselves in the boat. The girls do recommend that you practice with it at home before the race. It's evidently not that hard to use, but you'll want to have some experience with it before the race. We also packed Handi-wipes (Walmart, $2).

Having four people very close together in a canoe with many other paddlers close by called for some degree of privacy, so I brought along a poncho we could cover ourselves with while we were taking a bathroom break (in keeping with our dual use strategy, the poncho could have also been used in the event of rain). I believe we used this approach only a couple of times paddling to Lexington, but by Day 2 we could have cared less who we peed in front of, so it wasn't really necessary. Just let me say as a parent that there's nothing stranger than hearing your daughter fill up a container in the middle of the river on a hot day.

Instead of going in the boat, other teams pulled along shore, hopped in the water and did their business. It didn't take that long to do and got them cooled off as well. We only pulled ashore when we had to do something other than urinate. For that event I packed a lightweight plastic shovel/trowel and toilet paper. The procedure was to find a place along shore that's away from the river but is still readily accessible and not filled with poison ivy, dig a small hole with the plastic shovel, do your business, drop in the toilet paper and fill dirt back over the hole, and then clean your hands with Handi-wipes.

If you're in a kayak, things are a little tougher since you're so low in the boat. Going to the bathroom in a kayak might be something you'll want to practice on a lake, since depending on how you position yourself, it may cause the boat to tip.

Finally, there are some paddlers who forgo the niceties and just pee in their boat. When they get to the checkpoint they hop out and rinse the boat out and they're ready for the next time. We didn't quite see ourselves being that hard core, but it's certainly an option.

As you can deduce from the above descriptions, it would be a whole lot easier if you didn't go at all, but that would be a big mistake. As awkward as it is to go to the bathroom (especially when the paddler in the boat next to you is trying to strike up a conversation), it's a necessary part of the race. Not going takes two different forms: Either not drinking so you don't have to go, or holding it as long as you can. Neither approach is acceptable when you're paddling 340 miles. Make sure you hydrate well and accept the fact that frequent bathroom breaks are an important indicator of hydration and is a critical piece of your strategy for finishing.

Sun

With half of our crew being lifeguards, you wouldn't expect the sun to be an issue, but as with many other things to plan for in this race, you can't assume you could handle the sun in the same way you would on the lifeguard stand.

Think of a typical day in the life of a lifeguard. In at 11 a.m., put on sunscreen and start cleaning the pool. At 12:30 p.m., the pool opens and you work your first 45-minute shift. At 1:15 p.m. you're in the shade of the guard shack for your 15-minute break, get a drink and put on more sunscreen. By the time the sun goes down at 8:30 p.m., you've done another six shifts in the stand and applied sunscreen two to three more times. Total amount of sun exposure: approximately 7.5 hours, and after working a 3-day rotation, approximately 22.5 hours in the sun.

Now think about the MR340. Sun is up at 5:15 a.m. Tuesday morning, but you're not out until 6 a.m. Gun goes off, you paddle in the sun (no shade to be found). You hit Lexington that afternoon, and as the sun's setting you pull into Waverley around 8:15 p.m. Next morning you're on the water at sunrise, have a quick stop in Glasgow, and then make Katfish Katy's by sundown. Total time in the sun so far: 30 hours, and you're just a little over halfway.

Comparing a lifeguard's day to the MR340 really illustrates how long you'll be baking in the sun over the length of the race. Even for the lifeguards in our crew, that was going to be a long time catching rays. Add to the fact that Missouri, like the rest of the county, experienced record temperatures and drought in the summer of 2012, so we couldn't count on a break from the sun and heat. You really only have a few options to protect yourself from the sun. You can bring sunscreen and apply it as often, or you can cover up and not worry. We opted for full cover which consisted of the following items:

O'Neill Rashguard compression shirts (www.swimoutlet.com, $39 each): Having collected what seem to be a million t-shirts, we were familiar with the benefits of long sleeve polypropylene shirts but were concerned about the loose fit and the potential for the shirt to gather and chafe under our lifejackets. We had already bought our team shirts when we decided, after reading some rave reviews on the Rivermiles Forum, to purchase light-colored Rashguard t-shirts (light color to help reflect the sun's rays). Rashguards differ from traditional polypropylene in that they contain spandex, and thus are a much snugger fit than typical running shirts.

Although I was concerned about the tightness, the shirts worked out beautifully for a number of reasons: they were smooth enough that our life jackets could slide back and forth over them very easily, preventing chaffing and rub areas; they were long enough in the arms that they covered the back of the hand up to the glove preventing sunburn areas; and finally, they seemed to offer better evaporation properties which kept us cooler. (With a loose shirt, the sweat rolls down to a lower area and evaporates from there. With the Rashguard, because of its snugness, sweat evaporates where it appears, making the area of evaporation much larger.) Expensive shirt, but well worth the price.

Biking gloves (Kmart, $14): You normally wouldn't think of gloves for sun protection, but the back of your hands is a very easy spot to get burned if you don't cover it up or apply sunscreen. We read many threads on the Rivermiles Forum listing the pros and cons of using gloves. We took a very simplistic approach and decided to wear them with the theory that we could always take them off. But as it turned out, besides removing them every once in a while for a change of pace, the whole crew ended up wearing gloves throughout the duration of the race.

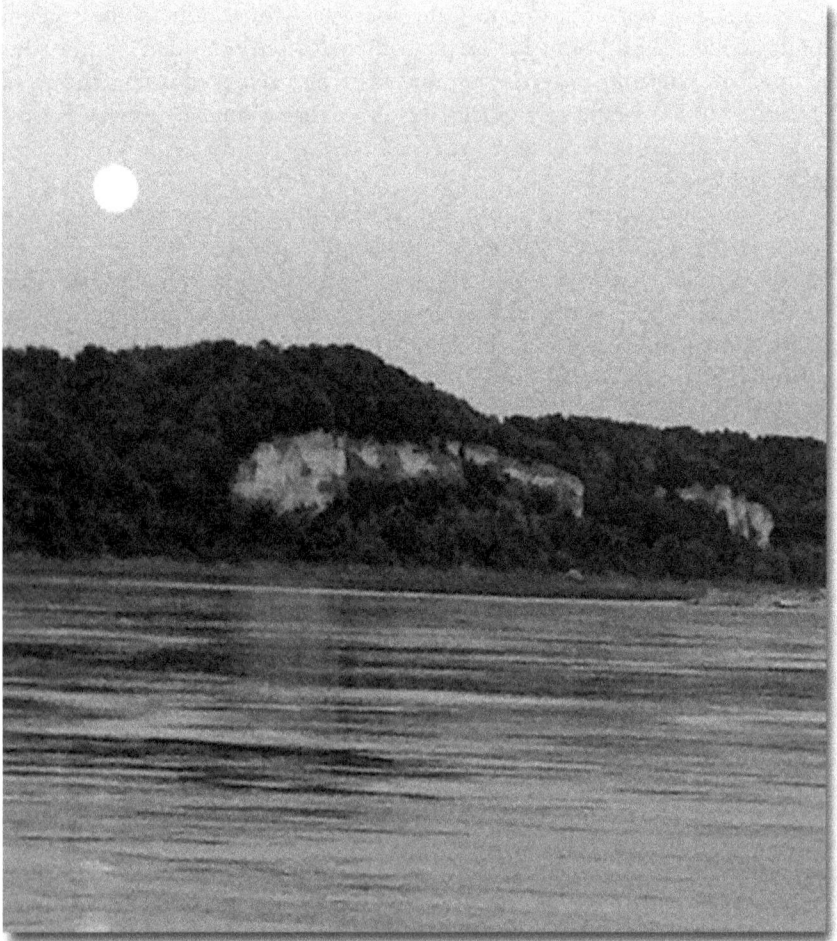

Moonrise doesn't always occur until after sunset. Here's the moon rising as we paddled toward Katfish Katy's Wednesday evening.

One place where we did have to watch was the thin strip of exposed skin on the back of the hand between the shirt and the glove. For this area we would apply some sunscreen every few hours during the day.

Nurse's scrubs pants (JCPenney, $5): Although not made from the most breathable material, you can't find a more comfortable pair of pants to wear if you're in a canoe. For kayakers, biking pants or loose fitting shorts work well depending on your preferences.

Polypropylene hiking sock liners (Cabela's, $11 a pair): There's nothing more painful than having the tops of your feet burnt. The sock liners were nothing more than a way to keep sun off of our feet without having to worry about wearing shoes. Although we weren't overly impressed (they were slick against the bottom of the canoe, always wet since the bottom of the boat was wet, and hard to get on and off), we're not sure what we would have used instead.

Water shoes (Walmart, $10): For water shoes, anything light will do (we'd rather spend the weight on more liquids). You're really not going to use them for much more than getting in and out of the boat, but for kayakers, you might consider a shoe with a stiff sole to better distribute your weight on the bracing pedals. Make sure you wear your shoes outside the boat. The ramps and areas are fairly clean, but all it takes is one sliver of glass or metal to make it a bad day. We considered flip flops, but having a closed-toe shoe provided better protection from potential foot injuries.

Wide-brim straw hat (Walmart, $9): You could use a baseball style hat, but we found that on the river during the course of the day, the sun will be coming at you from all different directions, so having a wide brim hat that covers around your head was beneficial. As with our shirts, we chose light colors in order to reflect off as much heat as possible.

Cheap polarized sunglasses (Walmart, $15): An absolute must on the river to minimize glare. We made sure we had lanyards just in case we went swimming.

Sunscreen: Although well covered, we did bring one bottle of SPF30 for our neck, face and back of our hands, as well as individual sticks of Chapstick (Walgreens, $3) with SPF15 for each of the crew.

One of the surprising sights for us on the first day was just how many people wore tank tops and shorts (almost to the point of making us think we did too much thinking). But as we got closer to Lexington, we saw more people with a reddish hue, making us feel more confident about our choice of sun prevention. We're sure they had good intentions for using sunscreen to start with, but as it is with hydration, you may not know you're in trouble until it's too late.

Food

Think about what you had to eat last week starting Tuesday morning. From Tuesday to Friday afternoon, you probably had four breakfasts, four lunches, three dinners, three afternoon snacks and four evening snacks.

Over the course of the MR340, you'll have food breaks at least that many times, with (if you're lucky) a 3 a.m. pancake stop in Miami thrown in as well. How you approach food goes a long way in sustaining energy and keeping discomfort to a minimum.

As we discussed with hydration, your first inclination is to think, since this as an athletic event, that you'll need to have plenty of Clif Bars, GU Energy Gel and quick energy Sport Beans on hand to complete the race. But read the back of any one of those packages and you'll notice that all of them are geared to provide quick bursts of energy over a relative short period of time. The thing is, this race isn't measured in hours, it's measured in days. While having a few on hand to provide a quick boost here or there is helpful, you'll really need a more sustainable food strategy than just energy bars.

Our approach? Eat normal.

While it doesn't sound nearly as exciting and exotic as what you'd think the world's longest non-stop canoe and kayak race should require, it works great as long as you have a Ground Crew to help.

Here's what we ate over the course of four days:
- Deli sandwiches bought from a Kansas City supermarket the night before
- Pizza from Papa Jack's Pizza in Lexington
- Fresh and frozen fruit
- Hamburgers
- Packaged powdered and chocolate doughnuts
- Deli sandwiches from a sandwich shop
- Arby's
- Qdoba
- Waffles (yep, and unbelievably delicious)
- McDonalds
- Pizza from Pizza Hut
- Fresh Old Town Donuts from Florissant, MO
- Snacks including Slim Jims, potato chips, granola bars, fruit chews, peanut butter cookies, Cheezits, Sweet and Salty Nut mix, cheese and peanut butter crackers and of course Goldfish crackers.

Doesn't really sound like an ultra endurance athletic event, does it?

While our food list looks a lot like what a teenager would down on a weekend, there was a method to our approach.

Think "light" before the race – The MR340, in the tradition of many marathon and half-marathon races, offers a pasta dinner before the race. Why pasta and not steak? Pasta is loaded with carbohydrates, which digest easily and provide efficient fuel to the body. Steak is high in protein, which is good for muscle building and repair but isn't an optimal fuel for racing. Protein in the form of steak also takes a long time to digest, meaning if you eat it the night before the race, you still may be carrying it with you a couple of days later. Because of this processing time, preparing for the race food-wise starts much earlier than dinner the night before. Ideally a day and a half before race time, you're starting to eat lighter, easily digestible foods such as salads, fruits, vegetables, yogurts, granola, fish and, of course, pasta.

We always liked to ask the question before we ate, "Do I want to race while carry this food inside of me?" While pre-race eating for the MR340 is not nearly as critical as preparing for a marathon (it's easier to paddle with it in you than run with it in you), good eating the day before helps set the stage for a good race.

Eat things that you know agree – There's something about trying something new and challenging that for some reason makes you want to include new and challenging food in that mix. For us, we went the safe route and kept to our comfort zone. Did we miss out on some great Boy Scout barbecue and stir-fry Thai? Absolutely. But we traded it for the knowledge that while we might have some surprises along the way, some sort of food reaction wasn't going to be one of them.

Hydrate and cool down while eating – On Monday night prior to the race, we went to the grocery store and bought a 2-foot long deli sandwich along with cherries and grapes, the thought being that the fruit would help with hydration. We realize now we should have taken this a step further like they did in Miami, where they sold sandwich bags of frozen fruit. Besides keeping you hydrated, it helps to cool you down as well (you could also use it instead of ice in your cooler). On a 104-degree day, food items that help cool as well as hydrate really help.

Make it snack size and waterproof – Although it created lots of trash that got strewn over the bottom of the canoe, having the snacks in individual serving bags worked very well for two reasons: First, your hands won't be the cleanest, so having individual bags makes it easy to open and eat without touching anything edible. Secondly, each individual snack bag is waterproof, so in the unlikely event you went swimming you'll still have some food left when you recover.

Because we have four crewmembers, we bought boxes of snacks at Sam's Club, and then had the Ground Crew grab handfuls to resupply us at each checkpoint. I did go a little crazy at first, where for some reason I packed enough snacks to feed everyone at the 8 a.m. start. (Exactly how many Slim Jims do you need?) While we paid a weight penalty for my attempt to ward off starvation, it probably only added a few pounds total. The lesson here is to take a hard look at the amount you're bringing since you have ample opportunity to get resupplied at the next checkpoint.

Eat in the boat – You'll hear over and over on the forum to not waste time eating on shore when you could be floating downstream on a 4-mph current while you're eating. That was absolutely our intent at the start, but as we progressed through the race we adhered to that strategy less and less. First off, it was just plain nice to get out of the boat and stretch. Secondly, it gave us a few minutes to swap stories with other teams and catch up with the Ground Crew.

It's important to note that we had this luxury for the simple reason that by the second checkpoint at Waverly we were ahead of the clock. We guarantee you there were teams that did everything in the boat because if they didn't, they wouldn't have made the cut-off times. Banking time early gives you lots of flexibility later.

Sure, we could have picked up 15 more minutes per checkpoint if we ate in the boat, but in reflecting back on our goal to finish well and meet great people, we did the right thing by taking food breaks onshore.

This is me getting welcomed by Leigh at Glasgow. Every checkpoint is marked by a flag and a flashing light along with lots of people, making them very hard to miss. It's helpful to know what side they'll be on so you're not on the opposite side of the river when you arrive.

Call ahead – One thing to consider is just how many food opportunities there are along the route that are accessible to the Ground Crew. We got into the habit of either calling the Ground Crew three hours or so prior to a checkpoint to discuss what we wanted ("Do you want cheddar melt with that Arby's Deluxe?"), or while at one checkpoint make plans for the next one ("Since we'll be hitting Klondike at 6:30 tomorrow morning, do you think you can bring us some Florissant Old Town donuts, coffee and chocolate milk?"). The advantage here is that if you get a hankering for KFC somewhere upriver from Boonville, there's a good chance your Ground Crew can make your dream can come true.

There's also good food at the checkpoints. One thing we wish we would have done more of is to make better use of all the volunteer food tents along the race. Except for Klondike, there were places to purchase food and drink at every checkpoint. For many of these organizations, supporting the MR340 is a major fundraising event, so if you have a chance to purchase something from them, know that it goes to a good cause.

Our challenge was that in many cases, since the Ground Crew didn't know what food or drink was being sold at each stop, they ended up purchasing food prior to arriving. When we do it again, we might try to go there first to see what they have, then make a determination on whether to buy there or go someplace else.

Stopping in Miami – One of the coolest places that pulls out the stops for the MR340 is Miami. In our quest to get ahead of the clock, we pushed on past Waverly Tuesday night, and ended up arriving in Miami around 2:30 a.m. Like something out of a dream with tiki torches, roped walkways and scented candles in the porta potties, Miami offered an unbelievable selection of food and drink. Our only disappointment was they didn't start serving pancakes until 3 a.m., and by leaving at 2:45 a.m. we ended up missing out on what we're sure was a great breakfast. If you have some time on the clock, taking a food (and potty) break in Miami is well worth the time spent.

But what if you have limited or even no Ground Crew? Here's where the Rivermiles Forum can help by identifying what checkpoints and access points have food and water. Be aware that there will be lots of changes right up to race time (Did the organization running the food tent try something new? Will they run out of something by the time you get there? Can you eat what they're selling?), so you'll need enough food and water with you to get you through those spots. Paddlers without a Ground Crew will pack more than we did and thus be more weight sensitive, so look at type of foods used for backpacking. They don't necessarily need to be freeze dried, but look for dried fruit and nuts, cans of tuna, chicken or stew, granola bars and other foods that are individually wrapped and that will last for the duration of the trip. That way you won't have to worry about having to eat these foods early when there may be some better alternatives at the checkpoints.

Instant meals like Ramen Noodles and freeze dried stews are also an option, but they may require hot water. We did pack a sterno stove and coffee pot, but ended up not bringing it with us in the canoe since we felt we could last through the night without coffee (actually, coffee was served in Miami). Leaving a water bottle out in the sun may get it hot enough to use without heating, but then again the noodles may be a little crunchier than you're used to.

Whatever the approach, remember that food is much more than just a way to keep alive through the race. Chosen well, the food you bring can help keep you hydrated, keep you cool and minimize "this sucks."

Paddle like a Female

There's no great mystery to why women have such a huge advantage in a race like this. Their secret? Camaraderie. I saw this first when I coached grade school track and volleyball. It took me a while to figure it out, but I realized that incorporating a social aspect to the team's training went a long way in enabling them to stick together, and push each other, as a group. But make no mistake, they could be friends and still compete fiercely.

Where that becomes an incredible advantage is not in the shorter events like marathons (hard to imagine a marathon being a short event), but events like the MR340 that are measured in days, not minutes.

An example from our race comes to mind. We pulled out of Katfish Katy's at 11:30 p.m. on Wednesday, bound for Jefferson City, 36 long miles away. A short distance down the river we came across two female solo paddlers, and before you know it we had ourselves a convoy all the way to Jefferson City.

Now that rendezvous in and of itself doesn't sound like much until you think of it in terms of "maleness." It was often a challenge to maintain the same speed as other boats during the race. Everyone has their own pace, but for us it was exacerbated by the differences in our 21-foot Kevlar canoe versus, say, a very efficient solo kayak.

So the choice for the women was clear: Smoke that sorry canoe filled with singing girls and their dad, or hang back and enjoy the company. And honestly, I say "choice" here, but I don't think it really ever occurred to them to sprint on past. They knew how powerful camaraderie was in a race like this.

Now put on your "guy" hat. You going to hang back and chat when you can put your head down and get ahead of them by a half mile by Jefferson City? Seriously?

That's what we mean by paddle like a female. Oh, and did they both finish? You bet.

Motivation

The last thing I'd like to cover as we finish up the Enduring section is motivation. I'm not big on motivation techniques, but they can play a powerful role in keeping you moving forward. People have all different ways they motivate themselves, from telling everyone at work they were going to make it and picturing the pain they'd feel when they had to tell them they didn't finish, to waiting until Hermann to eat that Clif Bar. There's no limit, but think about what motivates you, and reflect on it over and over before the race so it's there to strengthen you during the race. I can't finish discussing motivation until I share two favorite quotes I used often during our race:

"I don't have to, I get to." – Millions of people only dream about this race. We got to do it. Remembering this line always reminded me of how special it was to get to do an adventure such as this.

"Someday I won't be able to do what I'm about to do. Today isn't that day." – I saw this quote in a Runner's World magazine while training for my marathon, and it really put me in the right perspective during training to run 16 miles at night in the freezing cold. Five years and back surgery later, I remind myself that this day may be the day I can't run a marathon any more, but I'm glad I could run that day.

PART IV

CLOCK
MANAGEMENT

PART IV – CLOCK MANAGEMENT

You're safe, you're happy, now all you have to do is stay ahead of the cut-off times. Table 5 – MR340 Cut-Off Times lists each checkpoint's proscribed deadline.

Checkpoint	Mile Marker	Leg Distance	Cut Off Time	Average Leg Speed
Kaw Point	367	0	7 AM Solo 8 AM All Others	n/a
Lexington	317	50	5:00 PM Tues.	5.56 mph
Waverly	294	23	9:00 PM Tues.	5.75 mph
Miami	262	32	11:00 AM Wed.	2.29 mph
Glasgow	226	36	6:00 PM Wed.	5.14 mph
Katfish Katy's	180	46	12:00 PM Thurs.	2.56 mph
Jefferson City	144	36	7:00 PM Thurs.	5.14 mph
Hermann	98	46	10:00 AM Fri.	3.07 mph
Klondike	56	42	6:00 PM Fri.	5.25 mph
St. Charles	29	27	12:00 AM Mid-night	4.50 mph

Table 5 – MR340 Cutoff Times

   I was so focused on making sure we were ahead of these times that I had this chart memorized by the end of the race. This next section is focused on what you can do to make sure you, like us, are ahead of these cut-off times.

Be Efficient

It might seem strange to talk about being efficient in a section about staying ahead of the clock, but I put it here because clock time is less of an issue the father ahead of it you are, and an easy way to get ahead is to be more efficient. Think of it this way. Being 10% more efficient doesn't sound like much, but over the course of 88 hours it could result in an 8-hour time savings. Small, seemingly minor efficiency improvements, added up over 340 miles, can easily be the difference between making a cut-off time and not.

Speed between Checkpoints

When thinking of efficiency for the MR340, I think about speed and shore time. To get a better understanding of what I mean by these, let's take a look at Table 6 – Three Boatacious Blondes and Dad's Stopped and Sleep Times.

Checkpoint	Cutoff Time		Time Ahead of Cutoff	On Shore	
				Stopped Time	Sleep Time
Kaw Point					
Lexington	5:00 PM	Tues.	0:30	0:30	
Waverly	9:00 PM	Tues.	0:20	0:25	
Miami	11:00 AM	Wed.	8:30	0:30	
Glasgow	6:00 PM	Wed.	8:00	3:30	2:30
Katfish Katy's	12:00 PM	Thurs.	14:04	1:30	1:00
Jefferson City	7:00 PM	Thurs.	12:16	6:46	5:30
Hermann	10:00 AM	Fri.	12:40	1:40	1:00
Washington			---	1:00	0:50
Klondike	6:00 PM	Fri.	10:20	0:50	
St. Charles	12:00 AM	Midnight	10:50		
		Totals		16:41	10:50

Table 6 – Three Boatacious Blondes and Their Dad's Stopped and Sleep Times

The key ingredients in managing cut-off times are speed between checkpoints and time on shore. Of course they're related in that the faster you move from checkpoint to checkpoint, the more time you have on shore to do things like eat or sleep, and likewise the less time you have on shore, the slower you can go between checkpoints. With than in mind, let's first discuss speed between checkpoints.

Noticed the phrase I used wasn't "boat speed" but "speed between checkpoints." I intentionally phrased it like that because we equate speed to how fast our vehicle is going, when in reality it's how fast we traveled from Point A to Point B. Teams that paddle like mad for 20 minutes then sit and recover for 30 minutes very quickly get overtaken by teams paddling at a very slow, sustainable pace. Did the mad paddler beat the slow movers in a mile sprint? Yep, but too bad the race is 340 miles.

There's five major items that influence speed between checkpoints:

1) Weight – Weight is the one thing that has to be addressed before the race starts. We've already touched on weight from a perspective of an accumulated advantage, but unfortunately many paddlers discover they have a weight problem three hours outside of Lexington when they're already behind the clock and have no time or place to offload what's weighing them down.

When thinking about weight I remember how Philmont Scout Ranch handles the thousands of Scouts who bring all sorts of things that they think they'll carry over their 10-day trek. At Base Camp, the Philmont staff has everyone spread out on a table everything the Scouts plan to bring. Then the staff points out, item by item, the things that should stay and what should go. "You don't need seven pairs of underwear; get rid of some. You don't need five paperback books. Get rid of them," and so forth. It's a brutal process, but they'd rather have robust discussion on weight in the comfy confines of Base Camp than have a Scout crash and burn midway through the adventure because they brought too much stuff. Unfortunately the Philmont staff won't be in your garage when you're assembling your MR340 gear, so you and your team must make those tough decisions. Spend some time thinking about weight, then think some more. Unsure? Go ahead and bring it and let the Ground Crew hold on to it, at least for the first leg. They can always hand it to you when you get to Lexington (ahead of the clock, of course).

2) Pace – "Slow and steady wins the race." The tortoise finished and so can you by staying with a relaxed, sustainable pace. When I was little and went walking with my grandfather, we'd come to a hill and I would go sprinting ahead. I came huffing and puffing to the top as my grandfather caught up with me and said, "Start at the bottom with the same speed you'll be going at the top." And so it is with the MR340. Think relaxed. Think sustainable.

Is it possible that you're moving too "relaxed"? Sure, so my approach was to look behind us to make sure there were still people in back. My theory was as long as there's a group behind us, we were probably okay.

3) Paddling - Although you, like us, may have paddled many times before, one thing I wish we would have done is taken lessons. It might seem strange to think you'd need paddling lessons (how hard could it be?). It turns out there are subtle nuances to canoe and kayak paddling that make instruction worthwhile. My way of looking at it is this: If I could be 10% more effective in my stroke, that would have meant I could save 5,000 stokes over the course of the race (and some hand numbness as well). Many outdoor stores offer classes, and there's a number of instructional DVDs out there. The more efficient your stroke is, the more energy you have for later.

4) Path – You might be thinking, "It's a river, how important can a path be?" I thought so too until I saw teams wander from one side of the river to the other. The mile markers might have said 50 miles from Kaw Point to Lexington, but I'll bet if you measured some paddlers' path, their actual distance paddled would have been a lot longer.

So where should you be in the river? Stay dead center in the main channel. Let the river help you as much as it can by putting your boat in the right spot.

Staying in the channel turns out to be pretty easy. Take a look at your Missouri River map (A PDF file containing the Lower Missouri River Navigation Charts – Rulo, Nebraska to St. Louis, Missouri may be downloaded from the USACE website at http://www.nwk.usace.army.mil/ Portals/29/docs/civilworks/navigation/MoRiver_NavCharts_0-500.pdf. You'll only need Chart 25 to 89.) and follow the marked channel line. Just from the map you can see how it transitions from one side of the river to the other. I first thought that I would have to use a map to guide where I should be, but after awhile you get a sense of where the channel is and where it shifts. Barge pilots use channel markers along the river to tell them what's going to happen. Passing beacons are solid red triangle signs on the left side bank or solid green squares on the right side bank that let you know to stay on that side until you see a crossing beacon. Crossing beacons are diamond signs with red or green squares within them on the top and bottom that indicate that you should cross over to the other side of the river by aiming for the crossing beacon on the opposite shore. It might sound complex, but you'll be a real pro by the time you get to Lexington.

What's somewhat confusing about channel markers is that they are not telling you what your next move will be. They are actually telling you what move you needed to make to get to that marker.

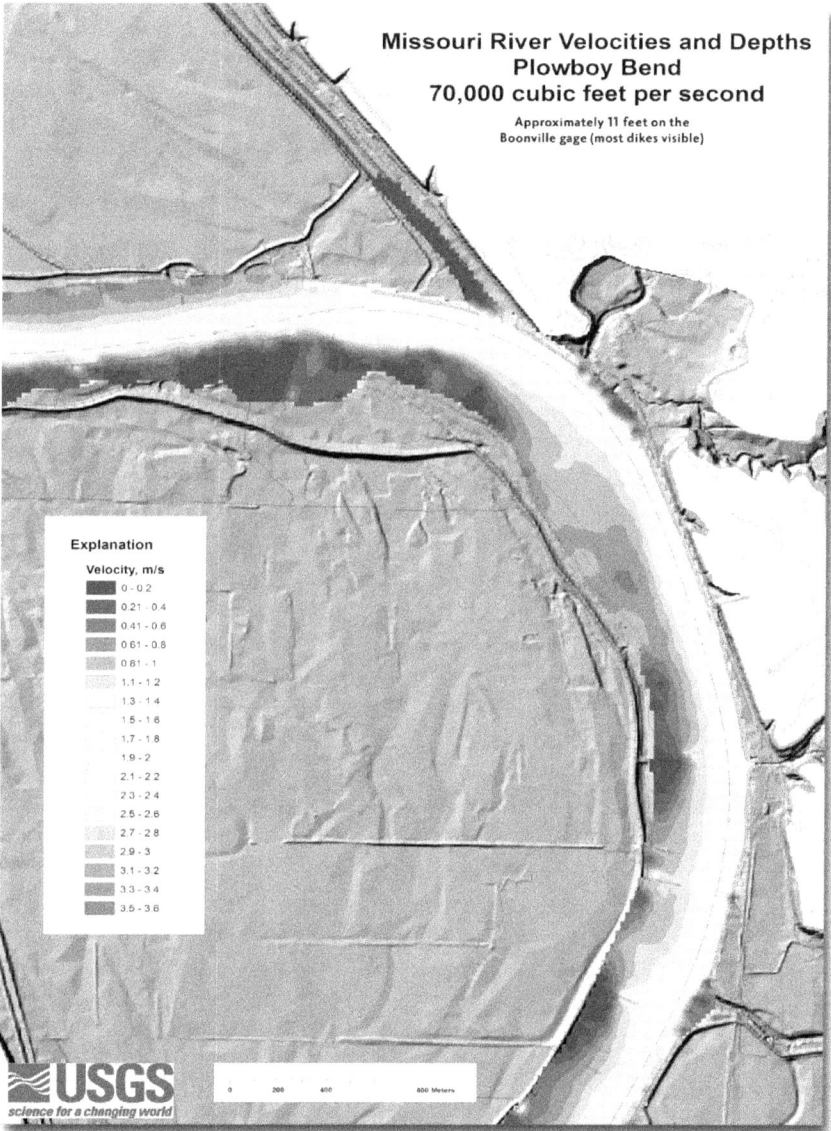

Missouri River Velocities and Depths
Plowboy Bend
70,000 cubic feet per second

Approximately 11 feet on the
Boonville gage (most dikes visible)

Explanation

Velocity, m/s

0 - 0.2
0.21 - 0.4
0.41 - 0.6
0.61 - 0.8
0.81 - 1
1.1 - 1.2
1.3 - 1.4
1.5 - 1.6
1.7 - 1.8
1.9 - 2
2.1 - 2.2
2.3 - 2.4
2.5 - 2.6
2.7 - 2.8
2.9 - 3
3.1 - 3.2
3.3 - 3.4
3.5 - 3.6

This map was produced by the United States Geological Survey and shows the water velocity over a two mile bend in the Missouri River. The dark area indicates slow moving water. The lighter indicates faster moving water, which is located in the main channel. If you hugged the inside portion of the turn, you'd find yourself in slower moving water in addition to having to dodge wing dikes. Staying in the main channel, while longer in distance, may potentially provide a 2-3 mph speed increase when compared to water near shore.

Say you're approaching a "passing" channel marker on the left side of the river. That means that the channel stayed on the left side of river from the previous marker. It doesn't mean that the channel will remain on river left. If you want to know your next move, you need to either find the next marker downstream (often a difficult thing to do) or turn around and look at the BACKSIDE of the channel marker. This sign will tell you your next move.

The reason this system exists is for barges with very powerful searchlights and very slow reaction times. It can be really hard for paddlers to see the next channel marker to find out what to do. The easiest thing is to turn around and look at the backside of the channel marker you just passed. If it's a crossing marker, that's what the channel will do next.

If you stay in the channel, by definition you're avoiding the wing dikes. That said, it's awful tempting to cut short a sweeping 5-mile turn by staying to the inside part of the curve. The problem is that although it may be a physically shorter route, it's harder paddling because it's outside the main current. You also run the risk of swamping by having to go over multiple wing dikes.

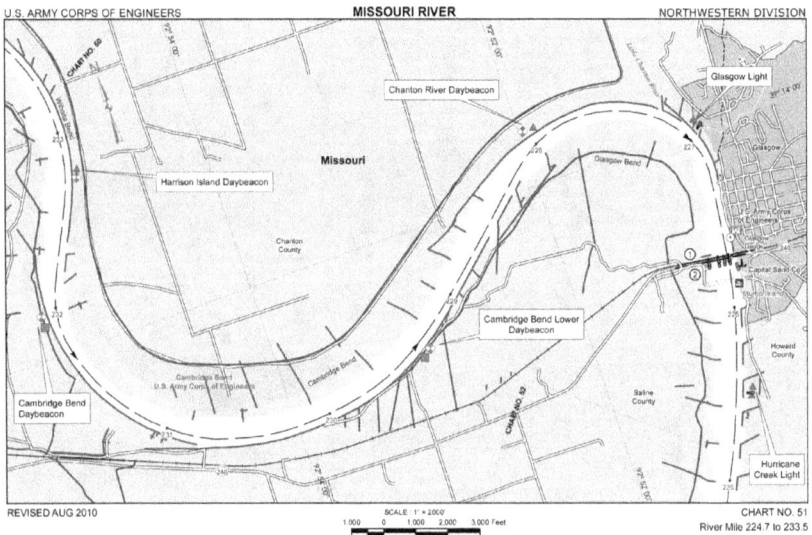

Here's a Missouri River navigation chart from USACE. Notice that the solid channel marker next to the Cambridge Bend Lower Daybeacon indicates that you'll have stayed on the right side of the river, but the channel marker next to the Charlton River Daybeacon indicates you'll be transitioning over to the left side of the channel prior to arriving in Glasgow.

Though we knew everything discussed above, we still didn't run the most efficient path throughout the race. Sometimes you can't see the mile markers from the main channel, and we would wander over to the shore just to see if we could get a glimpse of where we were. Other times we just plain zoned out paddling and then realized that we weren't in the optimum spot. How much time we lost by traveling further than we needed is anyone's guess. It's always a battle not to wander about.

5. Boat - Many people who quit early do so because their boat wasn't suited to the task and quickly decide they would do it next year in a better boat. There are, of course, determined paddlers who finish the MR340 regardless of their boat's efficiency. Then they come back next year with a better boat.

Time on Shore

Table 6 on page 82 also does a nice job illustrating how time on shore affects your cut-off time, and how your location relative to cut-off times affects your decisions about how long to stay on shore. Out of the 77 hours we spent on our journey, a little less than 17 hours were spent on shore. Of those 17 hours, around 11 hours were spent sleeping. So what did we do for the other six hours? The answer to that leads into the second key ingredient in managing cut-off times: Time on shore.

The whole purpose of being on shore is getting prepared to get back on the water as quick as possible. From an efficiency perspective, any task, action or movement that doesn't contribute to getting you back or sustaining you on the water quickly is wasted effort.

When we landed at Lexington, 50 miles into the race, we spent 15 minutes waiting in line for the bathroom. While it felt good to be out of the canoe walking around, it was probably 15 minutes of bathroom time we could have spent in the canoe. At Waverly we did the same thing, but at least it was five minutes faster and also included a shirt change. Glasgow was probably our worst spot in terms of efficiency. The bathrooms are located at the other side of the field, maybe 100 yards away. I can't tell you how many times I walked back and forth from the bathroom to the boat ramp in 104-degree sun. While the inefficiencies in Lexington and Waverly were caused by potty breaks, the last one was because by that time in the race, our van had stuff strewn from front to back, which meant there was no easy way for us to get everyone in and out. No room also drove us to sleep outside instead of in a nice, cool air-conditioned vehicle[3].

Now compare that with our next stop at Katfish Katy's. We got out of

---

[3] While a great idea to get paddlers cooled down, be careful of running a vehicle with the A/C blasting for hours. While we didn't have any problems, we heard of other Ground Crews whose vehicle overheated.

the canoe, walked up the hill, ate at the top, drove to the bathroom, got back in the car and slept, walked down the hill and paddled away. No wasted motion or energy walking around or waiting. Now that's efficiency. The difference, of course, is that we had three checkpoints' worth of practice to figure out the most efficient way to be ashore. At every checkpoint past Katfish Katy's we operated in the same efficient manner and, in keeping with our strategy to "finish well," we still had time to fit in conversations with other paddlers and crews while being efficient. Note that efficiency on shore doesn't end when you're ahead of the clock. Just because you're ahead doesn't mean it's smart to waste energy by being inefficient.

It would be fun to take a video of crews at the Lexington checkpoint, and then compare it with video of them in Jefferson City. I'll bet most of the teams, like us, were rough at the start but were a well-oiled machine by Jefferson City. The problem with this approach is if you're pushing close to the cut-off times, you won't get those opportunities to "practice" like we did at the early checkpoints. Doing it again, I think we'd hit the ground running without much thought. As a first timer, you'll want to spend some time with your team choreographing your time on shore. What specific tasks do you need to do on shore to get you ready for the next segment of the race? Is there anything you can do in the boat now (i.e. potty) that enables you to not do something on shore? What does the Ground Crew need to do to support you at the each checkpoint?

Your Ground Crew plays a pivotal role in your time on shore. When your rear end is screaming bloody murder, it's hard to get motivated to get back in the boat. Besides resupply, it's their job to push, cajole or throw you back in the boat. Unfortunately when you minimize time on shore it doesn't leave a whole lot of time to catch up. We found that spending some time talking on the phone while you're on the river was a good way to catch up on events and plan your next checkpoint. That way you don't have to compress 20 minutes of coordination into a 2-minute sound bite while they're trying to throw you back in the boat.

Just by looking at Table 6 on page 82, you can see there were lots of places both on the river and on shore where we could have been more efficient, but by Glasgow we were ahead of the clock, enabling us to continue paddling a relaxed, sustainable pace and to spend more time on shore for things like eating and sleeping. But how did we end up almost eight hours ahead by the time we made Glasgow, the third checkpoint? The answer: Clock strategy.

Clock Strategy

In order to develop a clock strategy, understand how the course cut-off times are laid out. Looking at Table 5, the average leg speeds for both Lexington and Waverly are fairly quick but dip almost 3 ½ miles slower going into Miami. The reason for the lower average leg speed is to allow for sleep time. This slow-down in average leg speed also occurs going into Katfish Katy's and Hermann.

So based on the course checkpoints, is it okay to stay in Waverly Tuesday night, and then get up early the next morning for Miami? Not really. According to Scott, no team that has left Waverly Wednesday morning within the past four years has finished the race. That's because even if you make Miami in the nick of time, you still have to race to Glasgow in order to make that cut-off.

There's also the distance to consider. If you decide to take a rest in Waverly, you've only paddled 73 miles the first day. In order to finish you'll have to travel an average of 89 miles for the next three days, meaning your easiest day was the first day. It reminds me of an interview I read about the Hall of Fame Cardinals pitcher Bob Gibson. Someone mentioned he looked like he got stronger the more pitches he threw in a game. He told them there was no way he got stronger as he pitched. It was just that he was able to manage and overcome his tiredness. His mental toughness, not his raw physical strength, got him through the late innings. You will never be any fresher in the race than on Tuesday. That's the day you'll need to press forward and get ahead of the clock.

So got it, make it past Waverly, but to where? Here's where the flexibility part of the strategy comes into play. Hills Island is a huge sandbar located between Waverly and Miami. Since it tends to be above water for most races, MR340 staff builds a big bonfire to let paddlers know it's there and there's room to rest. Or you can go farther down the river and sleep in Miami. Or you could go farther still and shoot for sleeping the next morning in Glasgow. What you decide and when you decide it will be based on three key factors: how tired you are, your comfort with paddling at night and the availability of sleeping equipment.

I've read a number of postings where paddlers bed down for a few hours in Waverly, only to be awakened every 15 minutes by a train roaring through town. By the time they decided enough was enough, they'd wasted a couple of hours that might have been better spent paddling to a quieter spot. But even if you're in a quiet spot, it's wasted time to lay awake because you're not ready to sleep. So your first clock strategy decision will be at Lexington and again at Waverly, asking, "When do I think I'll be tired enough to stop?" We knew we'd have to be unbelievably tired to sleep through noisy trains, so we planned to keep paddling until we were really sure we'd sleep, which lead us to the next decision: "Do we want to paddle at night?"

The reality is you're going to paddle at night. There's no way you're going to perfectly time your arrival at checkpoints to coincide with the setting of the sun. The funny part is, the transition from dusk to nighttime is so gradual; it's 11 p.m. before you finally say, "Hey, it's night." But even that doesn't last for very long, because soon after the sunset the moonrise begins and it's light again. Plus you'll have 200 of your closest paddling buddies right there with you.

The last decision is sleeping equipment. Sleeping at Hills Island gives you a jump on the morning, but it's inaccessible to the Ground Crew, meaning you'll have to carry all your sleeping gear. If you decide that Miami's the place to rest (i.e. you're tired enough that you can sleep through a train), the Ground Crew can be there to meet you, but you need to be concerned with their well being as well as yours. As we stood and talked in Waverly, we decided that we'd be able to catnap in the boat and we'd be okay paddling at night, so we decided that we wouldn't bring any sleeping equipment nor would we have our Ground Crew meet us in Miami. That meant they'd be able to sleep for seven hours or so at their Boonville hotel while we handled the next checkpoint by ourselves. It was that clock strategy that allowed us to make it to Glasgow by 10 a.m. the next morning by virtue of passing up sleep in both Hills Island and Miami.

Consider what that decision meant. When we landed in Glasgow, we were already eight hours ahead of the cut-off, meaning we had time to sleep somewhere other than our boat. If we would have stayed in Hills Island or even Miami, we'd be much closer to the cut-off time by the time we made it to Glasgow. While it's true we had been paddling off and on for more than 26 hours by the time we stopped in Glasgow, at no time did I feel we were in an unsafe condition. It was at 8:45 p.m. Tuesday when we finally made the strategic decision to get ahead of the clock. Would I recommend pressing ahead given you were safe? Absolutely. Would we do it again the same way? We'd try, for the simple reason that we might not feel as good as we did last time around, but we would make sure we had the flexibility to adjust if necessary.

Being ahead of the clock opens up multiple opportunities, but it's your clock decisions made on Tuesday that will set you up for a successful finish.

Sleep Strategy

Sleep is one of the hardest parts of the race to survive without and then write about. What makes it so difficult is that most of us have never gone for that duration with that little of sleep. Most people have pulled "all nighters" writing a paper or stayed out late. We probably crashed fairly soon after, so the sleep deprivation we're familiar with is less than 24 hours, not 88. And if you're like us, you're probably not going to practice any hard core sleep deprivation skills prior to the race. Which means that unlike all the other skills, equipment and strategies we've talked about so far, everything discussed about sleep is going to be theoretical until you actually get out there and experience it at race time.

Sunset on Wednesday night. Over the four days of the race we encountered three sunsets and sunrises while on the river. Each one was as spectacular as the next.

But do you really have to sleep? Wouldn't it just be easier to just keep going and sleep at the end? Here's where eons of evolution rears its ugly head. It is possible for a solo paddler or team to cross the finish line in 40 hours with no sleep.

Is it possible for solo paddler or teams to hit the finish line at 60 hours with no sleep. Not likely.

Is it possible for solo paddler or teams to hit the finish line at 88 hours with no sleep. No way.

Sleep and "this sucks" are two different things. In our experience, too much "this sucks" makes you quit, but lack of sleep makes you extremely inefficient and plain unsafe.

Our team's approach to sleep was twofold. First, we made sure we had multiple sleep plans so whether we were in the boat or on shore, we could get some shut eye, and secondly, we were flexible enough to adjust our game plan based on the weather and how we felt as opposed to what we had originally planned for months earlier.

We're sure there were teams out there that had planned way in advance to sleep in Waverly for a couple of hours, then start again before daybreak toward Miami. But what if they came paddling in to Waverly still feeling pretty good? If they weren't ready for sleep and lay awake during their allotted sleep time then the break was wasted. They may have been better off to take that break in Miami or Glasgow, but rigid adherence to their original plan didn't give them the opportunity.

Another factor that drives the need for flexibility (as well as good clock management) is weather. Take advantage of the unexpected advantages of storms, fog and heat. While you would usually not use "storm," "fog," "heat" and "advantage" in the same sentence, there may be times it's smarter and safer to be on shore than on the water. Make sure you're ready for these opportunities.

Not having encountered that level of sleep deprivation before, we kept our sleep strategy very fluid with only one absolute, a hotel room in Jefferson City. But why a hotel room? Why in Jefferson City?

To be honest, after reading about people dropping out because they couldn't escape the gravity of their hotel bed, I was very concerned that the same thing could happen to us. But since there were some real benefits to a hotel (namely a shower and quality sleep in a quiet, air conditioned room) it was just too good to pass up.

But where? Many paddlers reserve hotel rooms in Marshall, then have their Ground Crew shuttle them from Miami to Marshall for a break (approximately 15 miles one way). While the distance to the hotel isn't bad (we'd rather spend more time sleeping in a bed than in the car shuttling back and forth), the real problem is that at that point in time in the race, the cut-off time isn't too far behind. By stopping at Miami, we'd run the real risk of missing the cut-off time further in the race by not banking time upfront.

Glasgow would be a good spot for a break, except that there are no hotels in Glasgow. Boonville was a possibility, with hotels and a casino close to the water, but it's past Mile Marker 200, which would be close to 28 hours into the race at our 6 mph pace. For us, Boonville would be too far to get to with no sleep, yet too close to use it as a second stop.

But past Boonville, you run out of hotels until you get to Jefferson City. So the strategy we developed was to sleep on shore somewhere between Waverly and Glasgow, then hang on until we got to Jefferson City.

I also had an ulterior motive in waiting until Jefferson City. We live in St. Louis and have been to Jefferson City many times, so we mentally connected "Jefferson City" with "close to home." We took training runs starting in Hermann, so I felt if we made it to Jefferson City, the pull of the finish line would be enough to keep us moving. I'm not sure that would have been the case if we stopped in Miami or Boonville.

And while it didn't really factor into our decision, there was another slight problem with hotels in Marshall.

No rooms.

Due to the high demand from the other paddlers and Ground Crew, all rooms were booked. Many teams book their rooms the instant they hear the dates for the next year's race, so be aware if your strategy includes Marshall, it will be impacted by availability. But before you book your reservation in Jefferson City for a race six months from now, let's re-address the concept of flexibility.

Based on our training runs, I thought we would be paddling at between a 5.5 mph and 6.5 mph pace. That pace, however, was only based on 4-hour morning training runs near St. Charles, not in the heat of the day on a different part of the river, so in reality I had no clue what our actual pace would be.

That's where simple math takes effect. The addition of 0.5 mph doesn't seem like much, but over the course of 340 miles it makes a world of difference. By paddling at 5.5 mph, you'll get to Lexington at 5 p.m. (right at the cutoff time). If you paddle at 6 mph, you'll get there when we did, at 4:20 p.m. That's a 40-minute difference and it's only the first checkpoint. Besides speed, it'll also be difficult to project how you're feeling. Maybe you're ready to stop, and then again maybe not, but you hate to stop just because you reserved a hotel room.

The key to our shore sleeping approach was to keep it simple and quick. We considered a tent since many teams had used them with great success, but the logistics of it left much to be desired. It would have to be big enough to sleep four, so it was hard telling if the Ground Crew could find a spot at a checkpoint, much less set it up and take it down in the dark.

There was always the option of carrying a tent along in the canoe, but besides the weight and having the same setup and takedown challenges, we'd also have to find a piece of sandbar or bank in the middle of the night on which to set it up.

And what about the heat? Having slept in a tent when it was 100 degrees out, being inside wasn't the best place to be to get rest. So there was always the possibility of setting it up then not be able to sleep in it.

After much consideration (some would say over-thinking), I decided to go for a "tent lite" approach. What we'd have wasn't a tent at all, but an 8-foot by 10-foot utility tarp we could attach to the canoe and either sleep under or on top of it. The tarp also had the advantage that it could be used as a rain fly in the event we had to hunker down in a storm or wanted some relief from the sun.

One thing I learned in Boy Scouts was if you got a new tent, make sure you set it up before the trip. With that in mind, I spent a few hours one weekend prior to the race figuring out what was the best method to set up sleeping arrangements. My original plan was to flip the canoe over, tie the short side of the tarp to the boat, then extend the tarp out to the boat's side.

While the concept worked in principal, in reality all of our stuff would have gotten dumped when we flipped the canoe over. I finally opted for leaving the canoe upright, tying the short side of the tarp to the gunnels and staking the opposite ends down with two lightweight stakes. Keeping the canoe upright meant stuff inside would be exposed to rain, but we already had that covered by carrying everything in waterproof containers or bags.

Since the height of the canoe was fairly short, I brought two small aluminum tent poles to raise the height of the tarp (I never could find a simple way to use our paddles as poles). I made sure all the roping was attached to the fly, and then bundled up everything together. To complete the sleeping ensemble, we also brought along four lightweight yoga mats. While not as long or thick as camping pads, they would take up much less space in the boat if we decided to use them.

Up to this point, our book has been focused on safety, enduring and clock management. Ultimately these three sections come together at race time to get you to the finish line. Let's now follow our race adventure to see how well we did incorporating these areas.

PART V

Our MR340
Adventure

PART V – OUR MR340 ADVENTURE

Training

This is the embarrassing part of the book. As a dad, I sometimes find as I give my kids lectures about something that one of them asks, "What did you do when that happened to you?" and I can only respond with a mumble since what I did when it happened isn't the thing I'm lecturing them to do.

And so it will be with training.

We did not have near the amount of specific Missouri River training that I would have liked to prepare for this race, but make no mistake, we had many types of adventure experiences that helped us be ready. Besides hiking, camping, running and other sports we've participated in, we've also as a family paddled the Boundary Waters, been on a whitewater rafting trip, and canoed and kayaked many of the Ozark streams in Missouri. Based on those experiences I would classify us with intermediate level canoe skills. But paddling on a lake north of Ely, Minnesota, or on a small Ozark stream in southern Missouri isn't the same as paddling the mighty Missouri River, so over the course of two years each of the individual girls and I paddled on different segments of the river between Hermann and St. Charles, one of the last being a 4-hour trip in 100-degree heat. The longest paddle trip I had been on prior to the MR340 was a 42-mile canoe trip on the Meramec between Robertsville State Park and St. Louis. We might have been intermediate canoers on other bodies of water, but we were beginners when it came to the Missouri River.

My girls more than made up for their lack of Missouri River experience with their athletic prowess and mindset. Ellen's a good runner and an "Insanity" workout guru, and Christine was a state qualifier in the 500-meter freestyle swim. These two gave our team more than enough gas to get to St. Charles. Claire's in a different category. While not what I would call athletic in the mold of Ellen or Christine, she has a type of grittiness and determination you don't see very often. She's not in the front, but she hangs close to it.

And then there's me. I've been a runner for years, and after finishing two half-marathons the prior October, I had a disk rupture in my lower back and was operated on in mid-December. Recovery was slow, but I focused on walking, swimming and Insanity and by early summer felt good enough to attempt the MR340.

I provide our background not to brag. Although we were light on specific training, we had an extensive history of outdoor adventures on which to draw and an average to above-average athleticism. Through our trip to the Boundary Waters and Mount Elbert, we already understood and had competency in things like preparedness, safety, pace, hydration, clock management and sleeping. Using us as a benchmark to compare your team to us can help you formulate a training strategy like, "If the Three Boatacious Blondes competed the MR340 at this level, what specific areas should I focus on and what types of training should I do to develop additional competency I now lack?"

All is not lost if you haven't yet had a previous big adventure on which to draw. Should you run out and book a quick trip to Mount Elbert, then to the Boundary Waters with a quick white water rafting trip on the side? Not at all. But if you don't have experience in doing something outdoors over a period of a couple days that takes some level of preparation, part of your training regiment might be to try an adventure weekend to get the feel of the process.

The training I suggest isn't organized the same way as training for a half-marathon. Instead of saying things like "Paddle twenty miles at two times race speed," it's more of a checklist of things to help you fill in the blanks. A potential flaw in this approach is that it assumes you have a level of self-truthfulness that allows you to acknowledge your shortcomings and you have the will to address them. In the last few generations we've moved away from a focus on competency and towards a "as long as you feel good about yourself" approach. ("My kids do poorly on math, but at least they have great self-esteem about it.") My purpose here is not to argue societal changes in America but to point out the simple fact that the Missouri River could care less about how you feel about yourself or if you make it or not. The river might allow you to finish if you demonstrate the correct level of preparedness and competency (and even then it's not a sure bet). And it's not just that the Missouri River doesn't care. What I love about the great outdoors is that it's the ultimate "don't care" sounding board. It is your responsibility to care about nature, not vice versa. Recognizing the fact that there's a natural tension between how we might have been raised and what the river demands is the key ingredient in understanding how to successfully train for the MR340.

With that in mind, I've divided up the training into a number of sections which address both the athletic and competency aspects of the race. Remember that all members of your team should participate in the training.

Conditioning – This race isn't about power, it's about days and days of arm and trunk movement. With that in mind, I focused my training on my core and arms. For core workouts, there are two approaches. The first approach is the one I've done for years while training for runs. I combined six different core exercises (planks, crunches, superman, etc.) into a timed routine. For example, at the beginning of the year I would do each of the exercises for 15 seconds, and then complete three sets. As time progressed

I'd extend both the duration of each exercise and the total amount of sets I'd do each day. The nice thing about this approach is that it only takes 15 minutes or so and you can do it in your living room.

The other option is to have "Insanity" or "PX90" beat the hell out of you. These types of high intensity core workouts are absolutely brutal (they're probably outlawed by the Geneva Convention), but if you stick with them for the prescribed 90 days or eight weeks, you will definitely see improvements in core strength and flexibility and aerobic conditioning. A word of caution: While these workouts do a good job of getting you in shape, if you're over 40 you need to be very sensitive about injuries. Part of the allure of a workout like "Insanity" is that, well, it's insane. Although that sounds really cool, you get no points injuring yourself prior to the race. Whatever workout you decide to do, the point of it is to prepare you for the race, not break something so you can't race.

Linda has since started using Jillian's "Ripped in 30" which still has the intensity but is a much lower impact workout than something like PX90. There's lots of DVDs out there. But whatever you pick, stick with it and you'll soon see results.

For arm workouts, I swam. Swimming does a good job of combining conditioning with arm and core. My problem is I suck at swimming, so much of my early workouts consisted of not drowning which shouldn't be confused with a good workout. There are lots of other options besides swimming. Make sure you're focused on the upper body and arms as opposed to the legs. We met a solo paddler who talked about how he worked out regularly on a treadmill. While that was certainly better than nothing, his time in the gym might have been better served by working more upper body. Mixing in different workouts is also helpful. When you start getting bored with one type of workout, search on the Internet for other ideas. There's lots of interesting types of workouts out there.

Boat – Training in a boat, preferably the one you're going to use for the MR340, builds familiarity and confidence. Our problem was lack of access. We don't personally own a canoe or kayak, so our only opportunities to paddle were to tag along with Mike Claypool and his family, or to go to a lake in a local park and rent canoes for an hour or so. Not having access means you'll need to schedule specific dates for workouts. Scheduling was made even tougher for us since both Ellen and Christine worked as lifeguards most weekends. Next time I would have everyone plan their work schedule around scheduled paddling dates. When scheduling your boat workouts, don't forget to look at local paddling events. Your local adventure or canoe and kayak clubs are probably doing something every weekend in the summer, so check out their schedule and see if you can tag along.

Training with a partner other than your race partner is still valuable and is a good way to get in time on the river when not everyone is available. The Rivermiles Forum is a good place to look for other paddlers training on the Missouri. Many have the same problem we did with partner availability, so watch for paddlers looking for a temporary paddling buddy if yours isn't available.

Equipment – You need to be familiar with every piece of equipment you plan on carrying, including how to set it up, how to change batteries, how to reload or resupply. Plan on being confused, tired and muddled when you use this equipment. Practice with them now. You don't want to be somewhere downstream of Miami in the middle of the night replacing batteries only to find out you need a screwdriver.

Crew – We were very lucky in the fact that our crew all lived in the same house, which made it pretty easy to check up on each other's progress. If your crew is spread out, have regular discussions, checking in to see how everyone's training is going and to discuss recent postings from the Rivermiles Forum. At race time, you and your crew will be a tightly bound team whose success depends on one another, so having ongoing discussions prior to the race is a good way to motivate as well as assess progress. Also use these discussions to track commitment. If you have a paddle mate who's half in and for whatever the reason isn't committed to the adventure, it's better to know sooner than later.

River and Outdoor Experience – I saved the river and outdoor experience for last. If you're within reasonable driving distance of the Missouri River, plan on paddling a section of it with your crew. Make it a distance where you get a true flavor of what the race is about. Use this part of the training as a gut check to make sure you and the rest of your crew won't be quitting at Lexington because it wasn't what you thought it would be.

Over the last few years there have been a number of river races that have emerged all across the country. If you have any doubt in your mind, or you suspect your crew members' level of competency of commitment, you owe it to yourself to sign up for one of these races as part of your training. While you might not have the same boat and maybe all of your crew won't be able to make it, it's still a great opportunity for a check ride prior to the main event. The other benefit of participating in river events like the Kawnivore 100 or the Race to the Dome is that you'll be surrounded by people who have either completed the MR340 or are like you and are about to attempt it. There will be an incredible wealth of knowledge at these events and they occur early enough where you'll have time to implement and adjust prior to the MR340.

Race Preparation

Here's our suggested preparation schedule. The dates are somewhat flexible except for three: Sign Ups, Work Outs and Race Day.

January 1
- Sign up
- Start a MR340 Race binder

January to April
- Start working out
- Assemble equipment list and figure out what you have, what you can borrow and what you need to buy
- Start reading the Rivermiles Forum weekly
- Book hotel for the Monday night prior to the race in Kansas City

April to May
- Continue work outs
- Finalize boat selection, how you'll obtain it and transport it
- Finalize Paddling Crew
- Finalize Ground Crew and support vehicle
- Schedule summer outdoor paddling workout sessions with as many of the crew as possible

June
- Continue work outs
- Continue outdoor paddling sessions
- Re-review equipment lists
- Print out Ground Crew Guide and start binder for them
- Print out river navigation maps
- Reconfirm crew and boat selections
- Participate in a local canoe or kayak races

Early July
- Continue work outs
- Continue outdoor paddling sessions
- Reconfirm crew availability
- Develop and document paddler and Ground Crew race strategies

Two Weeks before Race
- Obtain all borrowed equipment
- Last call for purchasing equipment through mail order.
- Assemble checklists for race
- Assemble all boat, personal and Ground Crew equipment and boat. Re-assess weight. Confirm stowage placement.

Leaving for Kansas City

Here's where your lists come in handy. Assemble all the lists you've put together while you've prepared for the race, then check off each item as you load it in the car. Since we were using our minivan as the Ground Support Vehicle, I tried to group things together in separate plastic trash bags so we wouldn't have to go digging around when we loaded the canoe. I also made sure to personally check each of the girl's bags to make sure they had their compression shirts. Most anything else we could get from Walmart in Kansas City if we had to, but not the Rashguard compression shirts.

I did my final "dad check" to make sure nothing we needed was left, and off we went to Kansas City.

Many of you may be renting your boats near where you live and will need to transport them to Kansas City. If you're not used to transporting boats (and even if you are), make sure it's tied down securely, and take it for a test drive around the block to make sure it won't shift or slide. The canoe we rented was delivered to us, so transporting it to Kansas City was the first time we loaded it on our minivan. A canoe of our size makes for a huge sail, so don't be surprised if your vehicle drives differently than usual if you have a big boat on top.

On the way I pulled over a few times to check the ropes and to make sure the boat was still secure. If I sound paranoid, you're right, but the boat was one thing I didn't want to lose. It's another thing that couldn't be replaced at Walmart.

One of the coolest parts of our trip over from St. Louis was seeing all the other canoes and kayaks heading the same direction, many with a MR340 Finisher sticker on their back window. With more than 1,000 paddlers and Ground Crew, it's a sizable pilgrimage that heads to Kansas City come Monday morning.

Our first stop after we arrived at Kansas City was to drop by Kaw Point and unload the canoe. Kaw Point was a beehive of activity with many teams unloading their boats as well. Rivermiles provides security at Kaw Point, but obviously can't patrol everywhere along the river. I felt pretty safe leaving our empty canoe there for the night along with everyone else's, but if you have any concerns, bring a lock and chain and attach your boat to a tree. Two good spots to launch your boat at Kaw Point are from the boat ramp and from the point (if you're looking from the parking lot, the boat ramp will be on your right, the point on your left). We opted to launch from the point, so we left our canoe closer to the left side of Kaw Point.

After dropping off the canoe, we headed over to the MR340 check-in to get our race packet. If you're not fired up at Kaw Point, I guarantee you will be during check-in. There you'll find some of the greatest people you'll ever want to meet.

Besides picking up your race package and Spot Tracker, you can also purchase MR340 cups, hats, shirts and visors. Bring along some extra cash for these purchases. Although they'll also have them at the finish line, buy what you like during check-in because there's no guarantee what you like will still be in stock by the end of the race.

We were able to stay at Ground Crew Member Leigh's house in Olathe, Kansas, so we headed over there prior to the safety meeting. I read where there were a number of teams that slept at Kaw Point, but I'm not sure if the location was quiet or comfortable. Monday night will be the last time for three or four days that you'll have a soft bed and a warm shower, so wherever you overnight, pick some place you'll get a good night's sleep.

We had a light dinner of salmon and salad at Leigh's house. The hotel where the check-in took place offered a nice, pre-race pasta dinner. Kansas City has some great restaurants, especially bar-b-cue, but wherever you eat, be smart knowing that whatever you decide, it's coming along for the race.

Safety Meeting

The mandatory safety meeting is part safety briefing and part revival. In that ballroom, you'll be alongside of more than 1,000 wonderful paddlers and Ground Crew, from world class competitors to first timers, all trying to do that same thing you're going to do. We had team shirts made for the meeting and fit right in with teams wearing tuxedos, Hawaiian shirts and masks with capes.

It's exciting, but you still need to attend to business. Make sure both you and your Ground Crew bring a notebook. The MR340 staff will review river conditions, hazards, weather forecasts and other key safety concerns. Most importantly, note on your river map the locations of barges, sand dredges, chutes and other features. Location will be given by mile markers so they'll be easy to mark on your map.

The racing staff will also note any known land issues for the Ground Crew. Many times bridges will be closed for construction, or there will be detours. Take good notes. If you're still not sure, ask after the meeting. Your Ground Crew missing the Glasgow checkpoint won't help you finish.

The safety meeting usually doesn't last for more than an hour, giving everyone plenty of time to get some rest before the start. Before going to bed I made sure and removed my wedding ring to give to Linda. Your hands will swell over the course of the race and by the time you realize your ring is bothering you, it might be too late to get it off.

Race Start – Kaw Point (Mile 0)

Mile Marker:	367
Leg Distance:	0
Cutoff Time:	n/a
Time In:	n/a
Time Ahead of Cutoff:	n/a
Time Out:	8:00 AM Tues. (7:00 AM for Solo)
Time Stopped:	n/a
Time Sleeping:	n/a
Weather Conditions:	Clear and Very Hot (104 degrees)

If the Monday night safety meeting was about excitement and anticipation, Tuesday morning is all about focus. We arrived at Kaw Point around 6:15 a.m. and found a place to park just before the flood wall. There's a parking lot between the flood wall and the river, but we avoided the congestion by parking where we did and only added another 100 yards to our walk.

Solo paddlers start first, at 7 a.m., so if you're with a team, give the solo paddlers room to move and launch. You'll have plenty of time to get set after they take off. You'll be nervous, you'll be excited, but waiting for the race to start is a perfect time to relax. It was surprising how many teams were already in the water at 6:30 in the morning paddling about, 90 minutes before their start. Relax, save your energy. You'll have plenty of time to warm up over the next three or four days.

While we waited for the solo paddlers to start, we loaded all our gear, filled the water jugs and coolers, and got everything set up in our still land-bound canoe. Making sure everything's just right is much easier on shore than when you're in the water (although it makes for a much heavier boat to carry and launch). We placed everything we needed into the boat and only kept out the life jackets and other things we planned to wear. After the Star Spangled Banner and the start of the solo paddlers, we carried our canoe down the rocky trail to the point, pushed it out into the water and then pulled it alongside the shore where we could climb in. There wasn't that much of a line, but make sure you leave plenty of time to launch. Access from the shore will be dependent on the river level, so make sure and scout out how accessible your boat will be once launched.

Besides all the equipment and liquids stored in the small coolers, I also opted to bring along two 10-pound bags of ice that were stored in separate cooler bags. In one of those bags we put in our sandwiches and fruit, and the other just held ice. I also brought along a clear shopping bag where we placed all the snacks. The ice was probably overkill, but because of the heat

I was very worried about someone (namely me) overheating, and having the ice available on the boat allowed us to quickly remedy most heat-related problems.

Launching a heavily packed boat in a crowded river is an awkward endeavor at best. Try to get as many hands as you can to carry your boat, and don't drop or drag it against the rocks. Dings and scratches increase frictional resistance (punctures and cracks even more so). Paddling 340 miles is hard enough with a smooth, streamlined boat, so don't make it harder from something you can prevent.

Standing alongside your boat provides you one last time to pull out your checklist and make sure everything you planned on bringing is there and set up the way you want it. Did you pack enough water? Is everything tied down securely? Do you have enough Slim Jims to feed all of Lexington? I mention the last question tongue in cheek, but it actually is a good example of a planning malfunction on my part. My lists did include bringing snacks, but what I failed to consider is how many snacks to bring. What I should have had on the list was "five Slim Jims per person per segment," instead of saying "Snacks." This might seem like overkill, but the second lesson to take away is that you won't have time to think at the start line. Between the thousands of things flashing through your head and the hundreds of other paddlers getting ready to race, there's not much thinking done right before the gun goes off. Make your lists as detailed as possible so you know <u>exactly</u> what goes in your boat.

Secondly, look around at all the other racers to see what they're doing that you're not. It may seem late in the game to think about changing your plan, but having a Ground Crew enables you to easily make Walmart runs and make quick updates at the next checkpoint. Although we had already started by the time we noticed this, many of the canoes had leg cushions made from water noodles (Walmart). They had bought noodles with a hole in the middle, cut off 3-foot sections and then made a 3-foot length-wise cut, making a "C" shape. They then wrapped this around the gunnels so the paddlers' outside portion of their knees were cushioned by the noodle and not resting on the hard metal gunnels. Great idea, so we called our Ground Crew, explained what it was, and they had them ready by the time we hit Lexington. There's thousands more of these ideas. It's never too late to take some time and see what others are doing.

Finally, spend a few minutes with your Ground Crew to review your game plan:

What's the weather prediction and radar look like between the start and Lexington? Do both you and they have the right equipment? For us, the weather predictions for the whole week called for clear but hot (104 degrees), so our challenge was not surviving rough weather, but surviving baking heat over the next four days (that's why we had so much ice). Yours may be different, so spend some time discussing and thinking about how it might impact you plan.

When will you call to check in? What phone should you call? We planned to call one hour ahead of the checkpoint or sooner if we needed them to do a Walmart run.

Does the Ground Crew know where the next checkpoint is and how to get there? I had a map of Missouri with all the checkpoints noted. I also typed in all of the checkpoint locations in the GPS, but they still had to make sure they knew the sequence. Don't assume the Ground Crew will figure it out, because they'll be stressed as well just keeping track of you.

What specifically do they need to do at the checkpoint? What things would they need to bring from the car to the boat ramp? The Ground Crew might have to park a long way away from the boat ramp, so knowing what they need to bring saves on what might be some long walks. Linda brought along a wheeled cart to help move supplies, but even with that, multiple trips would have been a hassle.

Are there any personal safety checks you'd like them to do? Because of the heat I wanted Linda to check each of our water containers and drinks to make sure we were getting enough liquid. I also wanted her to keep an eye on everyone to make sure they were coherent and to head off any emerging problems or safety hazards.

We finally couldn't stand standing there any longer, so we hopped into our canoe around 7:30 a.m. and paddled across the mouth of the Kaw to wait for the race to begin. Sitting there quietly in your boat with all the other racers around you is a very special time. By the time you're in the water, all those months of preparation and planning are complete and it's time to focus on execution. Be sure to take a look around at that moment. What you and people around you are about to attempt hasn't been done by very many (my guess is less than 3,000). This is a very special group of adventurers so savor the moment. After the start you'll be too busy trying to finish to think very much about the uniqueness of this event.

Suddenly the cannon fires and you're off. The first couple of minutes or so is very hectic, but just relax. Your mission for the first 500 meters is to get into the mighty Missouri in an upright position. Many of the paddlers will be pushed to the right side of the Kaw which causes some bunching as they transition into the Missouri. We opted instead to aim for the left or upstream side portion of the Kaw and ended up having a lighter trafficked approach as we transitioned into the Missouri.

When I was training for my marathon, the team I ran with spent weeks and weeks working on pacing, the coaches' theory being that the pace you start with should be the pace you finish with. They cautioned us over and over to stick with the pace game plan, especially at the start of the race when there's a big tendency to start out fast because of the excitement and nervousness. If your first mile is 8:10 and your pace should be a 9:30, I can personally guarantee it's only a matter of time before it's a bad day.

Many marathon and half-marathon race organizers recognize this and had evolved into a corral type of start where groups of runners with the same pace are "corralled" into a specific order and location at the starting line. Race planners have even gone so far as to assign race numbers by corral. The great thing about this approach is that you can see where you're at not only by time but by what runners are around you at any given point in the race.

Not so with the MR340. It's quite possible that the paddler floating next to you at the start has plans on finishing in less than 50 hours while your goal is to finish. Pacing is further complicated by the simple fact that most of us don't know what our pace should be. Unlike training for my marathon, the very first time we were in that boat with that team and that equipment was at the start of the MR340. My own estimates ran from 4 to 7 mph, which is a range so big it's not that useful. So how do you pace yourself?

Our approach was to relax. Your heart shouldn't be racing, you shouldn't feel fatigued, and you shouldn't be developing blisters or cramps prior to the first checkpoint. The 50 miles between Kaw Point and Lexington is nothing more than an opportunity to relax and get in the groove for the rest of the race both mentally and physically. When I think pace, I think about the solo paddler who needed two IV's. Maybe he finished and maybe he didn't, but getting into his situation that early in the race is something you want to avoid at all costs. When you get to Lexington, you've might have survived 50 miles, but you still have 290 miles to go.

I have found with running, hiking and paddling that everyone tends to have a certain pace where they're most efficient. Where people encounter problems is when they speed up or slow down this natural pace due to excitement or the desire to keep up with someone else. You'll see this play out during the race. You'll paddle up to someone to say "hi" and see how they're doing, and after 10 minutes or so you'll feel yourself drifting ahead. Fifteen minutes later you'll be a couple of hundred meters ahead. They're at their efficient pace and you're at yours and everyone will vary.

For us we paddled at an almost exactly 6-mph pace. If we plotted a speed chart, I'll bet we didn't vary that speed from 5.7 to 6.3 mph during the entire race. It was relaxed and comfortable, but more importantly it was sustainable. But knowing what your pace is isn't the same as forcing yourself to keep a specific pace based on clock time. We never said, "Let's speed up, we're only going 5.6 mph." Instead we paddled at a comfortable pace and we noticed our consistency thanks to the GPS.

Our equipment worked perfectly. The shirts, hats, sunglasses, gloves, pants, socks and Personal Floatation Device (PDF) wore well and kept us cool as could have been expected on a 104-degree day. I grabbed some ice from one of the bags and passed it around to the girls. No one had any heat issues besides the fact it was unbelievably hot. Around noon we munched on our sandwiches and fruit. Between that and the plentiful snacks, we had more than enough to keep us going.

Checkpoint 1 - Lexington (Mile 50)

Mile Marker:	317
Leg Distance:	50 miles
Cutoff Time:	5:00 PM Tues.
Time In:	4:30 PM Tues.
Time Ahead of Cutoff:	0:30
Time Out:	5:00 PM Tues.
Time Stopped:	0:30
Time Sleeping:	None
Weather Conditions:	Clear and Very Hot

We felt pretty good going into Lexington, having started to pass solo paddlers two hours prior to the checkpoint. I made a phone call to the Ground Crew six miles out (one hour away) to make sure they were ready. We paddled up to a very crowded waterfront at 4:30 p.m. Teams were able to spread out along the shore as opposed to having to pull in at the boat ramp, but the shore was muddy as all heck which made getting in and out, plus resupply, a challenge.

One thing to think about when landing is that the river bank is very steep, so while it may only be a foot deep at the bow, it might be five foot deep or more at the stern (especially for us with a 21-foot canoe). I always asked the people helping land the boats if we were okay to get out. I figured they had worked it long enough to know what's deep and what's not. The other thing we paid attention to when landing was to make sure whoever got out first (usually Christine in the bow) straddled the bow to stabilize the boat so it didn't turn over. Her mission was to keep it steady until everyone was out.

Linda bought a couple of pizzas and handed us the boxes. I felt somewhat guilty not partaking in the Boy Scouts' amply supplied food tent, but Linda, not knowing what was there, bought the pizza in town prior to arriving. Most of us ate while she and Leigh resupplied the boat. Lexington had nice bathrooms, but we spent 15 minutes in line. We should have pottied in the boat and only used those bathrooms if we had business we couldn't take care of in the boat. But that said, it was nice to be on shore and walk around for a few minutes.

Resupply consisted of refilling all four water jugs from a 5-gallon water container, reloading Gatorade and waters in each of the four coolers, and picking up trash and leftovers from lunch. We still had lots of snacks and the rest of the pizza. Linda kept an eye on how much each of us drank by checking each of the liquid levels prior to reloading.

The team was back in the canoe at 5:00 p.m., right at the cut-off time except we didn't see the dreaded shag boat. Total shore time clocked in at 30 minutes, which was slower than what I expected.

Checkpoint 2 - Waverly (Mile 73)

Mile Marker:	294
Leg Distance:	23 miles
Cutoff Time:	9:00 PM Tues.
Time In:	8:40 PM Tues.
Time Ahead of Cutoff:	0:20
Time Out:	9:05 PM Tues.
Time Stopped:	0:25
Time Sleeping:	None
Weather Conditions:	Clear and cooling

This next section seemed to go by much faster. As the sun went down, the temperature fell. We hit Waverly right at dusk at 8:40 p.m. The boat ramp was very crowded, but we got lucky and came in right when somebody left. Linda and Leigh resupplied while we looked for the bathrooms (over the railroad tracks and up the steep hill) and changed out of our Rashguards and into t-shirts. We replaced the day bag with the night bag which consisted of a 136-lumen MagLite flashlight and light jackets.

A quick word on boat ramp etiquette – get on and off the boat ramp as quickly as possible. There will be many teams trying to do the same thing, so we made it a habit to get out of the canoe and carry it up out of the way before we exchanged pleasantries. Eat/talk/relax away from the ramp.

Remember that the boat ramps are not "reserved" for the MR340 but remain open to the public. This means that it's possible for a local to be launching his boat at the same time hundreds of paddlers are trying to land. It's great to see others using the river. We tried to be considerate and do what we could to work around their access needs.

Finally, be as quiet as you can at the checkpoints both day and night. Many paddlers sleep in the heat of the day (hint, hint), so we helped them get their needed sleep by being as quiet as we could.

Based on our speeds we expected to hit Miami between 2 and 3 a.m., which would have meant that the Ground Crew wouldn't have had much sleep time, so we decided to have them skip Miami, head to the hotel in Boonville and catch up with us the next morning in Glasgow. This meant, however, that we needed breakfast loaded as well as enough liquid to get us another 12 hours down river. We basically carried the same amount of fluids as we did earlier in the day, but I figured with the sun down we'd have more than enough to last us until Linda and Leigh met us at Glasgow.

Not having the Ground Crew in Miami also meant that we had to decide whether we would bring sleeping gear and the tent. We decided that we still felt pretty good and that we'd make it to Glasgow before we'd try and get some sleep. In the meantime we'd take turns placing our cushion on the bottom of the canoe and try to get a few hours of sleep.

Having made our plans, we turned on the bow and stern light and started heading downstream for Miami at 9:05 p.m.

Checkpoint 3 - Miami (Mile 105)

Mile Marker:	262
Leg Distance:	32 miles
Cutoff Time:	11:00 AM Wed.
Time In:	2:30 AM Wed.
Time Ahead of Cutoff:	8:30
Time Out:	3:00 AM Wed.
Time Stopped:	0:30
Time Sleeping:	1:00
Weather Conditions:	Clear and comfortable

This was by far the most spectacular part of the journey. The moon rose and provided more than enough light to see the curve of the river and the shore. As you looked down the river you could see a single trail of lights from the boats ahead, but you have to be careful not to put too much faith in their navigation. As we followed the boat in front of us we went over the edge of a wing dike. No big deal (as least as what we could tell), but it was a quick reminder not to assume the boat in front of you was in the channel.

Once dark we kept the music off so we could hear any rushing water (rushing water = bad day). Sound travels well across water, and it was very easy to tell from the sound where the wing dikes were. Christine kept the focusable MagLite and got into the habit of every five minutes or so scanning the river with the flashlight to see buoys. Most have reflective tape on them and show up a long way away. As you got closer you could hear the water rushing around them. I kept the second light with me and used it to help her or to take over when she was napping. We probably drove people in front of us a little crazy with the amount of times we scanned the river, but I had no desire to hit a buoy at night.

While Christine was scanning for buoys, she also scanned the shore for marker beacons. Once again we could see them a long way off, allowing us to keep in the channel.

It was about this time in the race I started to hate those mile markers. In many of the races I've run, one of my favorite mental games is to pretend that someone didn't put the mileage marker in the right spot (this happens more often than you'd expect for road races). So at times you can convince yourself that really you're on mile nine when maybe you are and maybe you're not. The problem with the Corps of Engineers is that, well, they're engineers and not only do they have a mile marker every mile, but every mile marker you see is EXACTLY 289...288...287. Each mile marker passed by every 10 minutes at a 6-mph pace. While doing the math for the next checkpoint was a nice diversion, knowing exactly where you were at all times was agonizing.

We started taking turns napping on this stretch. We pulled off our chair cushions from the seat, placed it on the bottom of the canoe, sat on it so our rear ends didn't get wet, and rested our head on the seat. There was plenty of time for everyone to get some shut eye, so we never had more than two napping at a time.

I felt great in my short-sleeve t-shirt, but Ellen ended up putting on a jacket. It was nice to have a set of clothes to choose from, although accessing the right ones in the dark was tricky.

You can get a little paranoid thinking you might miss the checkpoint in the dark, but the beacons at each stop plus all the boats on shore made missing one almost impossible.

We pulled onto a busy Miami boat ramp at 2:30 a.m. By this time the checkpoints will be very quiet since there will be many paddlers and Ground Crew trying to get a few hours of sleep. Let your Ground Crew know this as well. Slamming doors, radios and honking horns are tough on someone trying to sleep.

What especially struck me at Miami was that in the middle of the night, all these volunteers were doing what they could to assist the racers and Ground Crew. The man who helped us land our canoe had been in waist-deep water on the boat ramp since the first paddlers arrived hours earlier. I remembered him telling his friend to let him know when it was 6:30 a.m. since he had to head to work. Those volunteers are a special breed, and I always tried to thank each one for his or her efforts. Unfortunately we were so focused in Lexington and Waverly that we really didn't notice the number of volunteers. It takes lots of hands to run a checkpoint, so if you have a second, let them know how much you appreciate them.

After visiting the scented porta potties, we got a quick snack of hamburgers, frozen fruit, soda and coffee. Revitalized but sad we missed the pancakes which they don't start serving until 3 a.m. we hopped back in our canoe and headed downstream to Glasgow.

Checkpoint 4 - Glasgow aka "Pit of Despair" (Mile 141)

Mile Marker:	226
Leg Distance:	36 miles
Cutoff Time:	6:00 PM Wed.
Time In:	10:00 AM Wed.
Time Ahead of Cutoff:	8:00
Time Out:	1:30 PM Wed.
Time Stopped:	3:30
Time Sleeping:	2:30
Weather Conditions:	Clear and Very Hot (104 degrees)

It started off okay. We passed Hills Island where there was a large campfire and a number of paddlers taking a break and getting some sleep. We continued to take turns napping. The moon set and the sun rose. The miles clicked off, we ate our breakfast as the temperature started heating up and pulled into Glasgow at 10 a.m. It was here the racers started to stretch out. The ramp wasn't as crowded, and the checkpoint was more relaxed. Glasgow's boat ramp is on the edge of a pretty field with bathrooms and showers on the other side. Linda and Leigh met us at the landing, and we all piled into the van to find a shade tree we could sleep under. I pulled out the tarp and sleeping mats and everyone quickly fell asleep.

Two hours or so later I woke up in a pool of sweat. I walked back down to the boat ramp while Linda went to get the minivan so we could make a run for lunch. There on the ramp was a solo paddler, who had just loaded his kayak on top of a car.

"I'd done," he muttered. "It's way too hot out there."

Had I been in a better state of mind, I might have tried talking to him to see if I couldn't help him find motivation to continue. But instead, I slowly backed away, afraid I might catch what he caught.

It was my single worst moment of the trip. I expected better of myself and failed to deliver.

We left the girls sleeping while Linda and I drove into town for sandwiches. It was on this drive that the magnitude of what we were trying to do hit me. Twenty-six hours of paddling and we're only 141 miles in. Not even halfway. And we still have 100 miles to go to get to Jeff City...100 miles, ONE HUNDRED MILES......

I kept repeating that to myself while Linda got the sandwiches. 100 miles, 100 miles. 100 miles. I must have been saying it a little too much because Linda said, "It's not a hundred miles. It's closer than that." Ever so hopeful I pulled the mileage card, and there it was. Jefferson City was a mere 82.2 miles from where we were standing. It's odd to look back at that moment and explain the relief I felt, but somehow at the time a number like 82 seemed so much closer and, after my experience with the solo paddler, so much more in reach than a number like 100.

Linda and I drove back to the rest of the team in silence. Ellen and Christine were up, quietly sitting in lawn chairs. "So what do you think?" they asked each other. "So what do you think?" they asked me. "So what do you think?" they kept asking themselves.

Very rarely in life will you experience something exactly as you've thought about it for months and months. I knew this place would be the toughest part of the race. Glasgow[4] is far enough into the race where you understand the magnitude of what you're trying to do, but it's not far enough were you can see half way (much less the finish line). It was hot, we were tired, and we still had miles to go before we sleep.

But while unspoken thoughts rolled and twisted around in our hot and sweaty heads, not one of us was willing to open the door to DNF. It's okay to think about quitting, the key is being able to push those thoughts aside and find the will to keep going. And we did. Our team facing down the dreaded DNF remains one of my most proudest moments. Just as I imagined it would be.

But deciding not to quit isn't the same as getting in the boat. So I decided to drop the motivation bombshell...

"You know, Jefferson City's only 82 miles away. That hotel bed will sure feel nice."

That's all it took. We finished our sandwiches, loaded back into the canoe, and off we went down the river.

---

[4] **The good people of Glasgow have to wonder why their town gets such a bad rap with MR340 paddlers. It really is a pretty town. Too bad it's located in such a horrible spot in the race.**

Checkpoint 5 - Katfish Katy's (Mile 187)

Mile Marker:	180
Leg Distance:	46 miles
Cutoff Time:	12:00 PM Thurs.
Time In:	9:56 PM Wed.
Time Ahead of Cutoff:	14:04
Time Out:	11:30 PM Wed.
Time Stopped:	1:30
Time Sleeping:	1:00
Weather Conditions:	Clear and cooling

Back on the river, we were different. Somehow we knew that we had passed the first big test. We were on our way and in the groove. And then came Captain Ahab…

The cruiser disappeared just as quickly as it came, and we were left with the knowledge of how fast things could turn. I found out later that where we almost got run over was at the downstream end of Lisbon Bottoms. I say "found out later" because this was the first segment of the trip where I didn't have my USACE river maps. I had printed out all the map segments from Kansas City to St. Charles, laminated them, and then bound them into sections which coincided with the checkpoints. That way I only carried maps for certain checkpoints as opposed to the whole trip. The good news about this approach is that it makes for a much smaller set of maps. The bad news is you and/or your Ground Crew needs to remember to switch them out at each checkpoint (which we didn't do at Glasgow).

Lisbon Bottoms is an area that has been a problem for racers in prior years during times of high water. It consists of a chute that cuts off a sweeping bend of the river. The chute had been cut through during the prior year of flooding but had been partially sealed off by the USACE with a rock dike so the river channel doesn't decide to move there. When we passed it, there was a small section of the Corps' dike that had water pouring through it. There was no way we were going to mistake that for the channel. But in earlier races when the river was up, this small gap was much larger, making it look like part of the main channel. The problem is, if paddlers get fooled into taking this route, it'll take lots longer since the water running through it doesn't flow cleanly back into the main river channel due to additional rock dikes to slow the water. Once you get into Lisbon Bottoms, it's awful hard to get back out. Channel shortcuts look shorter but never are. The faster way to get down the river is to act like a barge and stay in the main channel[5].

Areas such as these are discussed at the safety meeting. Be ready to make a note of the potential problem as well as the mile marker. Next time I'll just make the note on the laminated map (then remember to bring the map).

There was something else we learned on this segment as we paddled through Boonville early that evening. Across from Boonville on the west side is Franklin Island Conservation area with access to the river. A number of the teams were stopping to meet their Ground Crew there for a quick break, supplies and rest. It's one of the many locations on the Missouri River that, while not a checkpoint, provides paddlers access to their Ground Crew. During the 2004 Lewis and Clark Bicentennial, a set of maps were developed to mark Lewis and Clark campsites. They also marked Missouri River access points (www.rivermiles.com/forum/ YaBB.pl?num=1357573158). These points are much less crowded than checkpoints and may be better located time-wise for both Ground Crew and paddler breaks. Knowing where other access points are gives you additional flexibility in case of bad weather, need for sleep, equipment adjustments or if you just want to take a quick break.

Twilight found us under the Interstate70 Bridge, and for the first time we began to see cliffs along the river as we transitioned from the prairie into the Ozark hill country. As the sun set and sky darkened, thousands upon thousands of bats flew above us, out for their evening meal.

We arrived at Katfish Katy's at 10 p.m., welcomed by our Ground Crew armed with Arby's and Qdobas (a good Ground Crew picks up food from one location; a great Ground Crew picks up from two). Linda had driven through Columbia, and while somewhat out of the way, the food from Columbia tasted good. The boat ramp at Katfish Katy's is at the bottom of a steep hill, with the parking lot at the top. There, sitting at a picnic table, we ate our dinner and enjoyed the cool breeze.

After a quick visit to the bathrooms, the team hopped in our running minivan, and with the A/C blasting, got in a quick hour's sleep. We were back on the river, fed and rested, by 11:30 p.m.

---

[5] **It's not just Lisbon Bottoms where you can take a wrong turn. Just below the exit of Lisbon Bottoms is Jameson Chute, on the opposite side of the river. This chute has lots of wood debris, good for fish but bad for paddlers.**

Checkpoint 6 - Jefferson City (Mile 223)

Mile Marker:	144
Leg Distance:	36 miles
Cutoff Time:	7:00 PM Thurs.
Time In:	6:44 AM Thurs.
Time Ahead of Cutoff:	12:16
Time Out:	1:30 PM Thurs.
Time Stopped:	6:46
Time Sleeping:	5:30
Weather Conditions:	Hot and muggy (100 degrees)

Immediately pulling out of Katfish Katy's we met up with two female solo paddlers in kayaks and began to learn about teamwork. Up until that point in the race we were very self-centered. Part of that had to do with having a team of four, but the other part was that our pace was always slightly faster or slower than the other paddlers. What we soon realized as we paddled with them was that even though it might have been a slightly different pace, having someone to talk to and hang with was a powerful advantage. Simple things like seeing buoys or mile markers or wing dikes were so much easier when you had an extra pair of eyes. But the best advantage of all was the ability to pass time through conversation. Talking always seems to make time pass and keep you paddling.

During the previous night, we never saw much light besides the moon and our fellow paddler's stern light. But as we paddled toward Jefferson City, we found we could see the glow of the city when we were still hours away. At first you get excited when you start seeing the glow, but the happiness starts to evaporate when two hours later the glow is there and you haven't arrived. We began to see another glow on the horizon and slowly realized that it was dawn breaking. What a beautiful sight.

We pulled into Jefferson City at 6:30 a.m. and met our Ground Crew, who had stayed at a hotel in Jefferson City overnight prior to our arrival. Jefferson City is on the south side of the river, the boat ramp is on the north side. We quickly hopped in the minivan, A/C cranking, and headed to the hotel. We finally got our waffles at the hotel breakfast bar and then dove into some nice comfy beds.

We woke up from our deep sleep around 12:30 p.m. Linda had talked with the hotel staff so we could check out late. We took a quick run through McDonald's drive thru and then headed back out to the boat ramp.

By that point in the race, there was no way we were not finishing. We knew we still had some time left to paddle, but there was no doubt we'd succeed. Looking at pictures now, it's easy to see how that attitude showed up in how disorganized we had become. Stuff in our canoe that had been neat and orderly at the start was now in a more "relaxed" state. The girls decided that they had missed enough of the sun and opted for shorts and no hats as we started for Hermann.

Chamois Rest Stop – Hot Dogs & Pasta

Late Thursday afternoon, downstream from where the Osage River joins the Missouri, we saw a boat ramp on the south side of the river and decided to pull over and see if there was a bathroom. As we pulled onto the ramp, there was another team getting ready to leave. Turns out they had just had dinner with their Ground Crew who was pulling a camper and following the team down the river. They, like the people we saw across from Boonville, were using maps that identified access points, which they in turn timed with dinner and sleep for the paddlers. What a great idea.

As we were leaving, one of the Ground Crew handed us some extra hot dogs and pasta. Once more it illustrated to me what a great group of people we got to meet. Revived with good food and conversation, we hopped back in our canoe and headed to Hermann.

Checkpoint 7 – Hermann (Mile 269)

Mile Marker:	98
Leg Distance:	46 miles
Cutoff Time:	10:00 AM Fri.
Time In:	9:20 PM Thurs.
Time Ahead of Cutoff:	12:40
Time Out:	11:00 PM Thurs.
Time Stopped:	1:40
Time Sleeping:	1:00
Weather Conditions:	Muggy but cooling

Besides seeing the bridge for what seemed like hours, our trip to Hermann was uneventful. It was here that I noticed the cell coverage being spotty, but we still had enough of a connection to call the Ground Crew. It's strange to look at the distance between Hermann and Jefferson City, and compare it to the trip from Kaw Point to Lexington. Lexington seemed like so much more effort than our paddle to Hermann, and yet they were nearly the same distance. Linda and Leigh met us at the boat ramp with a couple of Pizza Hut pizzas, which we quickly devoured while sitting at a covered picnic bench overlooking the river. We then hit the bathroom and jumped into the minivan for a quick nap.

Since we were getting fairly close to home, Linda and Leigh decided to head back to our house in St. Louis, and then meet us at Klondike with breakfast. Knowing they were heading home to sleep gave us an added push to get this race finished. After sleeping an hour, we were back in the canoe, heading downstream to Klondike.

Rest Stop – Washington

We would have been able to press on if we had to, but by 4 a.m. we were feeling pretty spent, and in keeping with our strategy to finish well, decided to take a quick nap in Washington which, like Hermann, has a wonderful waterfront area. There we found the bathrooms and picnic benches, some already covered with sleeping paddlers. We each crawled on top of a table to get a quick nap. As with many of the checkpoints along the route, Washington's pavilion is probably 20 meters from a very active set of railroad tracks. With mile-long trains roaring by every 15 minutes I can tell you we were so tired we slept through every single one. What a difference being exhausted makes.

Checkpoint 8 - Klondike (Mile 311)

Mile Marker:	56
Leg Distance:	42 miles
Cutoff Time:	6:00 PM Fri.
Time In:	7:40 AM Fri.
Time Ahead of Cutoff:	10:20
Time Out:	8:30 AM Fri.
Time Stopped:	0:50
Time Sleeping:	None
Weather Conditions:	Hot and muggy (100 degrees)

Klondike was probably my favorite checkpoint. We were in good sprits as we jumped back into the canoe in Washington, knowing there'd be coffee and doughnuts waiting for us in Klondike. As the sun rose we pulled into the checkpoint and to our amazement were greeted by over 100 paddlers. Turns out there was another paddling event taking place at the same time as the MR340, and this group was in the process of launching their boats when we pulled up. We were able to spend a few minutes talking with them while we ate our doughnuts and drank coffee. They were very interested in our journey and wished us luck as we headed out to the finish, again having had the opportunity to meet some great people.

PART VI

FIRST TIME
FINISHER

PART VI – FIRST TIME FINISHER

St. Charles (Mile 340)

Mile Marker:	29
Leg Distance:	27 miles
Cutoff Time:	12:00 AM Sat.
Time In:	1:10 PM Fri.
Time Ahead of Cutoff:	10:50
Time Out:	n/a
Time Stopped:	n/a
Time Sleeping:	None
Weather Conditions:	Clear and hot

I remember reading that there's not a lot of paddling done between Knondike and St. Charles because everyone's so exhausted, but we kept up a fairly good pace, no doubt powered by doughnuts and coffee. What made this stretch agonizing was the simple fact that it took forever to finish. By that time in the race I knew our pace like the back of my hand, and no matter how I calculated it we were going to get there around 1 p.m. What made it even harder was I knew no matter what we did we couldn't change the time. And so we paddled on and watched the mile markers click off. Often during this stretch we'd paddle up to another racer and share some stories about the race.

It was on this leg of the race where we saw our first barge. We had plenty of warning it was coming at both the Hermann and Klondike checkpoints, so it was a little anticlimactic when we finally encountered it. As you'd imagine, the barge was moving very slowly upriver (although they can really move going downstream), but instead of throwing a large wake it simply made the water all around us very choppy. What was funny was that the 100 paddlers who started in Klondike had caught up with us by that time, and while we (being paranoid) moved as far away as we could so we wouldn't swamp, the other paddlers bounced around trying to catch air and had a great time. It's all in your perspective.

This was our stomping grounds. At every bend in the river we saw another familiar landmark that let us know we were ever so slowly reaching the finish line. Soon we paddled under the Route 364 (Page Extension) bridge, also fondly known as "The Bridge of False Hope." While we knew what it was, evidently many paddlers think this is the final bridge (it was built fairly recently and doesn't show up on some of the older maps), only to have their hopes crushed when the finish line doesn't appear.

By 12:40 p.m. we could see the I-70 bridge and knew that the finish was just on the other side. We put in a call to the Ground Crew to let them know we were close. The pace quickened, and soon we passed under the bridge and saw the finish. For me, pulling up on shore was great relief. We met our goal to "finish well" with everyone in great shape mentally and physically. As we climbed out of our canoe and up the shore to celebrate with our Ground Crew, the one thing I remember most was thinking simply, "We made it. We made it."

The awards ceremony was a great way to end the race. We had arrived earlier that afternoon and had time enough to run home, shower and take a long nap. When this picture was taken the race course was still open, with paddlers still arriving up until midnight.

If at first you don't succeed...

The pictures were taken and hugs exchanged when I stepped back, Popsicle in hand, to take a look at the now muddy and messy canoe that successfully transported us 340 miles. As I stood there thinking about our journey, a man standing beside me started asking questions. How did your hydration system work? Did you like those paddles or do you wish you tried something else? Did Kevlar make a difference or do you think you could have done it in an aluminum canoe? As we spoke, I initially assumed he was someone's Ground Crew (he was way too clean to be a recently finished paddler) when he mentioned that he and his partner had stopped on the first day. I don't remember why they stopped or even if he mentioned it, but I remembered wondering as I spoke with him, if we would have had to quit the race, would we have had the gumption to travel to the finish and watch paddlers come in, much less ask them about how they did it. Then it occurred to me. This race is tough, it's brutal, and many don't make the finish line. But I believe the DNF only occurs when you don't sign up at 12:01 a.m. the following New Year's Eve for the next race. If you don't finish one time, you'll learn a great deal about yourself, equipment and race strategy that can be put to good use the next time. The quitting part only occurs when you don't apply that knowledge to make it the next time. So when that man I spoke with comes paddling into St. Charles next year, he'll not only have the satisfaction that he paddled 340 miles and finished the race, he'll also have the knowledge he did something many of us don't do enough – get up off the ground, dust himself off and take another cut.

Keep trying and learning and you'll make it. And be better for it.

PART VII

EQUIPMENT

PART VII – EQUIPMENT

Equipment List

The equipment list shown in <u>Table 7 – 2012 Three Boatacious Blondes and Dad Equipment List</u> reflects what we brought with us for our race with the exception of the large cooler (we had individual ones) and binoculars. We used three waterproof compression bags to store items. The Boat Bag contained our First Aid Kit, flashlight and other items that needed to be accessible in the boat at all times. We specifically bought a heavy duty clear compression bag since we'd be using this bag the most and being able to see through it makes getting things much easier and quicker. The Day Bag included extra shirts and other items we'd need in the day, the Night Bag contained the big heavy MagLite, jackets and sleeping gear (if required). We had two colors of bags so we could make sure we got the right bag at the right time (yellow for day, blue for night). It was one more thing we did to minimize thinking at checkpoints. Rotating items in and out of the boat is a very efficient way to race, but you need to check and double check to make sure the right equipment is there before you shove off.

	Quantity	Item	Comments
In the Boat			
□ □	1	Boat	
□ □	Per Paddler	Paddles	1 per paddler
□ □	1	Paddle (Spare)	Per boat
□ □	1	Bow Light	
□ □	1	Stern Light on pole	
□ □	1	Sponges	
□ □	As Needed	Bailers with line	1 to 2 per boat
□ □	As Needed	Cooler	1 small per paddler or 1 large per boat
□ □	1	10' Bow Rope	
□ □	1	50' Stern Rope	Tied to Cushion

☐ ☐	1	PDF Cusion	
☐ ☐	1	Laminated River Maps	
☐ ☐	2	Race Numbers	Affixed to both sides of bow
☐ ☐	1	Trowel	For on-shore bathroom breaks
☐ ☐	1	Reflective Tape	Affixed to both sides of boat
☐ ☐	Per Paddler	Cup Holders	
☐ ☐	As Needed	Tie Straps	
☐ ☐	Per Paddler	Hydration System	

Boat Bag

☐ ☐	1	Waterproof Compression Bag (Small, Clear)	
☐ ☐	1	First Aid Kit	
☐ ☐		5-10 small waterproof bandages	
☐ ☐		4 small round waterproof bandages	
☐ ☐		Small roll of duct tape	
☐ ☐		Small roll of waterproof first aid tape	
☐ ☐		1 roll of Rolaids	
☐ ☐		Small bottle of 30 SPF sunscreen	

☐ ☐		Bottle of Tylenol	
☐ ☐		Small bottle of Pepto Bismal	
☐ ☐		Small bottle of Insect Repellent	
☐ ☐		Anti-Diarrheal Caplets	
☐ ☐		Chapstick with SPF15 for each person	
☐ ☐		Band-Aid Advanced Healing Blister Cushions	
☐ ☐		Handi-Wipes	
☐ ☐		Body Glide Anti-Chafe Balm	
☐ ☐		Moleskin with small scissors or knife	
☐ ☐		Handkerchiefs	
☐ ☐	1	Flashlight	
☐ ☐	2	Cell Phones in waterproof case	
☐ ☐	1	Laminated Safety Card	
☐ ☐	1	Toilet Paper	
☐ ☐	As needed	Spare batteries	Usable for Bow, Stern and Flashlight
Night Bag			
☐ ☐	1	Waterproof Compression Bag (Large)	Make different color from Day Bag
☐ ☐	Per Paddler	Light Jacket	
☐ ☐	1	Spotlight	

☐ ☐	1	Tent	May not use depending on strategy
☐ ☐	1	Sleeping Mats	May not use depending on strategy
☐ ☐	1	Safety Glasses	For bugs
Day Bag			
☐ ☐	1	Waterproof Compression Bag (Large)	Make different color from Night Bag
☐ ☐	Per Paddler	Shirt	1 per Paddler
☐ ☐	1	8' X 10' Tarp	Use for shelter or sleeping
☐ ☐	Per Paddler	Poncho	1 per Paddler
Food Bag			
☐ ☐	1	Insulated Food Bag	Use 2. 1 in boat, 1 Ground Crew reload
☐ ☐	As Needed	Food for Leg	
Optional			
☐ ☐	1	GPS	
☐ ☐	1	GPS Mounting Bracket	
☐ ☐	1	Binoculars	
☐ ☐	Per Paddler	Canoe Seat	1 per Paddler
☐ ☐	Per Paddler	Cushion	1 per Paddler
☐ ☐	1	Radio/MP3 Player	
☐ ☐	1	Bubble Level	See if boat's level
☐ ☐	1	Flotation Noodle	Cut and use as cushion on sides

Personal Gear			
☐ ☐	1	PDF	
☐ ☐	1	Quick Drying Shirt	Recommend long sleeve
☐ ☐	1	Quick Drying Pants	Recommend long pants
☐ ☐	1	Quick Drying Undergarments	Use Polypropylene
☐ ☐	1	Sock Liners	To keep sun off feet
☐ ☐	1	Small Pen Flashlight	
☐ ☐	1	Whistle	
☐ ☐	1	Cash	Bring small bills for Checkpoints
☐ ☐	1	Space Blanket	
☐ ☐	1	Hat	
☐ ☐	1	Sunglasses with lanyard	
☐ ☐	1	Paddling Gloves	
☐ ☐	1	River Shoes	

^ Check if in boat for start

^ Check if packed for trip

Table 7 – 2012 Three Boatacious Blondes and Dad Equipment List

Table 8 – 2012 Three Boatacious Blondes and Dad Ground Crew Equipment List has the items carried by Linda and Leigh. There can be lots of waiting when on the Ground Crew, so having things like a lawn chair and umbrella makes things a little more comfortable in the hot sun or rain. One item that really helped was the wheeled grocery cart. This made moving items from the car to the boat ramp very easy. You wouldn't think there would be much, but the weight adds up when you include all the sports drinks, water and ice.

	Quantity	Item	Comments
Ground Crew			
☐ ☐	1	Cash	Bring small bills for Checkpoints
☐ ☐	1	Camp Chair	
☐ ☐	1	Umbrella or Pop Up Dining Fly	
☐ ☐	1	Tool Kit	
☐ ☐	1	First Aid Kit	
☐ ☐	1	Extra Batteries	
☐ ☐	1	Charger	
☐ ☐	1	Cell Phone	
☐ ☐	1	Cell Phone Charger	
☐ ☐	1	Binoculars	
☐ ☐	1	iPad	
☐ ☐	1	Wheeled Grocery Cart	
☐ ☐	1	Food	
☐ ☐	1	Coolers with ice, water & Gatorade	
☐ ☐	1	Ground Crew Binder	
☐ ☐	1	Plastic Bags	
☐ ☐	1	Toiletries	
☐ ☐	1	Map of Missouri	
☐ ☐	1	Suntan Lotion	

Table 8 - 2012 Boatacious Blondes Ground Crew Equipment List

What Boat Should You Use?

Fifteen seconds after clicking "signup" online, I realized I had no clue what boat we were going to use. And it took me until a month prior to the race to lock down the actual boat. While there was plenty of time left for me once I decided on the boat, the sooner you know your boat, the sooner you can incorporate it into all the other parts of your race preparation.

Those who had boats hanging in the garage may have a leg up on those of us who don't. But don't fall in love with using your boat for this race just because it's your boat. At minimum, understand its strengths and limitations before you decide for sure it's for you.

Take a look at what others used for prior MR340 races.

Looking at all the pictures of those who made it to St. Charles (see Cindy Hiles's pictures of the race at www.cindyhilesphotography.com), you'll quickly realize that boats of every size, shape, age and price range have made it to the finish line. Many were as you would expect: Canoes and kayaks. Other were just plain different, like the catamaran during our race that was paddled by a team of four. A menagerie of boats make it to the finish line.

But no single kind of boat is optimized for the MR340. While many of the higher performance boats used for the MR340 are variations of ones used for events like the Texas Water Safari (www.texaswatersafari.org/), as of today, none have been specifically designed for the MR340. So rest assured, when you show up at the start line with whatever you finally decide on, you'll fit right in, since there's really no "best" type of boat category.

So the question isn't "What kind of boat will make it to St. Charles?" It's "What boat best maximizes my skill set and comfort level for this race?"

For that answer, we'll need to look in the most unlikely of places – your high school physics book.

The Physics of Boats

It might seem to be a bit of overkill to be digging into physics when all you're really trying to do is find a boat, but understanding why boats are built the way they are goes a long way into understanding what boat is right for you and how it aligns with your race strategy.

For thousands of years, boat designers have followed some fairly simple laws of physics in order to optimize their design for specific uses. The key word here is "optimized." Just as a Chevy Corvette is designed to go fast but not go four-wheeling like a Jeep, boat designs optimize for maneuverability, speed or carrying capacity, often at the expense of other characteristics.

In physics, the Archimedes Principle states that the weight of the floating body must be equal to the weight of the displaced fluid, meaning that for every pound of weight you carry, you'll displace one pound of the water you're floating on. While one additional pound doesn't seem like much, it's one more pound of water you'll be pushing out of the way for 340 miles. Total boat weight (you plus equipment plus boat) does matter, so consider every opportunity possible to minimize weight, starting with your boat.

Boat weight is largely driven by the material it's made of (size being the other). Below is a comparison of tandem canoes using different materials:

o Grumman 17' Double Ender Aluminum: 75 pounds

o Wenonah Sundowner (17') Royalex Plastic: 67 pounds

o Pygmy Taiga Wilderness Tripper (17') Wood: 60 pounds

o Wenonah Minnesota II, (18' 6") Kevlar: 54 pounds

o Wenonah Minnesota II, (18' 6") Graphite: 42 pounds

You'd pay a 33-pound weight penalty if you decided to use aluminum instead of a graphite, so why would anybody use aluminum? The answer has to do with the durability. If you come to Missouri and paddle one of the many Ozark streams, your outfitter will more than likely provide you with either an aluminum or a plastic canoe. They're much more rugged and forgiving of all those rocks people hit. Sure, they're heavier, but not having a boat crack in half (Kevlar and Graphite are much more susceptible to cracking than aluminum) when it hits something is a good trade off.

If you head up to the Boundary Waters where rapids are fewer than the Missouri and weight plays a larger role due to portaging, many outfitters offer Kevlar (including the Wenonah Minnesota series). For them, offering a lighter canoe is possible because of the lower likelihood of damage from impacts.

What about the MR340? Certainly the Missouri River has its share of wing dikes and floating trees that could cause damage. Is lightweight okay or do you need something more robust? Here's where it comes down to personal preference. For our team, I felt we had enough canoeing experience on the Missouri River that we'd be able to avoid most hazards, so we opted for Kevlar instead of something heavier. However, I also made sure we were ready for the dreaded "gash in the side" by bringing along some duct tape. There's no perfect answer, but just remember you can lighten equipment and food as you go downstream, but you're not going to lighten your boat.

One thing you might have caught in looking at the boat lengths above is just how long these canoes are. A tandem canoe that's 18.5 feet long at first seems really long, especially if you've water-skied behind something shorter, like an 18-foot Sea Ray.

The difference between canoes and powerboats is their hull design. For boats traveling at relatively slow speed such as canoes, kayaks and paddleboards, displacement hull designs are used. For boats traveling at higher speeds (think ski boats), planing hull designs are used. Displacement hulls are designed to displace the water. Planing hulls are designed to ride on top of the water as they get to higher speeds. And as you might expect, displacement hull designs utilize a different set of physics than planing hulls.

When developing hulls, boat designers take into account another physics equation: Theoretical hull speed. A displacement hull's theoretical speed can be calculated using the following calculation:

$$\text{Hull Speed Velocity (in Knots)} = 1.34 \times \sqrt{\text{Length of boat's waterline in feet}}$$

Using the above equation, an 18.5-foot canoe has a hull speed of 5.8 knots (approximately 6.6 mph). How do you add more speed? Add more length. For example, a 20-foot long canoe at waterline would result in a hull speed of 6 knots or 6.9 mph. It's because of this length-to-speed relationship that you'll see some extremely long boats entered in the race.

The "Three Boatacious Blondes and Dad" loaded up and paddling towards the start line at the beginning of a hot, hot day. We're in full sun gear, wearing hats, sunglasses, long-sleeve shirts and pants.

However, there are drawbacks to length. While you'll see many long boats entered in the MR340, you won't see any at the Missouri Whitewater Championship for the very simple reason that they're hard to maneuver. For whitewater, you'll see canoes and kayaks with very short lengths since in those events paddlers are willing to trade off hull speed for the ability to quickly maneuver around rocks. On the Missouri River, you're able to see for a very long way, which gives you plenty of time to make your move.

While important, length at waterline isn't the only factor when it comes to speed. The interaction between your boat and the water also comes into play.

Imagine a friend on a mountain bike and you on a road bike. If you both started at the top of a hill and coasted down to the bottom, who would win? Having had that very experience, I can tell you my road bike won. Why? Because of its narrower, smoother tires, my road bike has much less rolling friction than the knobby tires of my friend's mountain bike, and thus I traveled faster down the hill.

For boats, instead of rolling friction between the tire and the ground, there's the frictional resistance between the water and the boat. Just as for bike tires, the smaller the surface area of the boat that touches the water, the lower the frictional resistance between the boat and the water.

This area of contact between a loaded boat and the water is called "wetted surface." Since the larger the wetter surface, the more frictional resistance, racing boats incorporate hull designs that minimize their wetted surface area. Designs such as this result in a long (for speed), narrow (for less wetted surface) hull.

Length also has an advantage in that it assists with the boat's holding track, or maintaining a straight line, when paddling. Shorter boats, while more maneuverable, don't hold track very well, so it requires constant paddle adjustments to keep them on course.

So the perfect boat is one that's light, long and very narrow, right?

Well, maybe...if you can handle it.

If we took these calculations to their extremes and build a very long but very narrow hull, we'd have something that would be very fast with low frictional resistance. We'd also have something that would flip over very easily.

Designers refer to this potential for flipping as "primary" and "secondary" stability. Primary stability refers to the boat's "tippiness" when sitting flat in the water. Boats with high primary stability feel solid underneath when getting into the boat, and boats with low primary stability feel skittish and, of course, tippy.

Secondary stability comes into play when the boat is turned on its side. Good secondary stability will help keep the boat from flipping all the way over. Poor secondary stability means that the boat will be very hard to prevent from flipping over once on its side.

Typically hulls that have high primary stability have low secondary stability (think recreational canoes that are hard to start the flip, but when they go, they go), and those with low primary stability have high secondary stability (think racing canoes).

The stability of the hull is a result of trade off between width (or beam) and shape (flat, half circle or vee) which are in turn determined by how much wetted surface area the designer was willing to incur. It can also be influenced by the height of the paddler's seat. A kayak with the same hull width is going to feel much more stable than a canoe of the same width since the kayak's seat is much closer to the water than that of a canoe.

While tippiness may not be such a bad thing (especially when a boat is more efficient due to a smaller wetted surface), it reminds me of a run I went on one winter. It had snowed the week before, so the trail I was on had lots of ice patches. As I ran over the ice, I tensed up and ran very cautiously. When I got home, I was tired and sore after running only a fairly short distance. It was, of course, due to how tense I was when running.

Unless you've had lots of practice, boats with low primary stability will affect you the same way. You may be able to go at a fast speed but could tire very quickly due to your constant reactions fighting the tippiness. You also have to worry about your reactions over the 88-hour race. Just because you're responsive enough at Kaw Point to keep the boat upright doesn't mean you'll be that way downstream from Hermann at 3:30 a.m. two days later.

Interestingly, there's an easy way to increase a hull's primary stability with outriggers (think Hawaii Five-O). These are thin, long, usually solid floats that are mounted in parallel on one side of the boat. Just as standing with your two feet shoulder-width apart makes you more stable than standing on one foot, outriggers stabilize the boat in both directions. Its flotation minimizes tippiness in one direction while its weight minimizes tippiness in the other.

Some boats are specifically designed with outriggers in mind. Other times you'll see them added to canoes and kayaks. In either case, the outriggers don't eliminate the need to balance the boat; they just provide additional insurance. Paddlers who use outriggers talk about "kissing the water" with the outrigger, because if the outrigger is digging too far into the water, the added resistance may offset the benefits of having a narrow hull in the first place.

The term "trim" refers to the levelness of the boat in the water. From a physics point of view, if the bow rides too high in the water, the boat will not hold track and tend to wobble side to side as you paddle. If the bow's too heavy, it'll dig into the water too deep, increasing resistance.

How trim comes into the boat selection discussion centers primarily around the weight of your partner(s).

If you're a solo paddler, your ability to trim the boat level is going to depend on where you stow your equipment. Since solo boats are already balanced, and most of your equipment will need to be within arm's reach, it's a fairly simple matter of balancing the equipment to achieve trim.

If you have a large crew like ours, keeping trim is a matter of ordering the paddlers and equipment in such a way as to evenly distribute the weight. For our team, I was the heaviest at 180 pounds, followed by Christine, Ellen then Claire, so in our canoe, we put Christine up in the bow, followed by Claire, me, then Ellen. Many racing canoes also provide an adjustable seat in the bow that slides forward and back by approximately a foot, providing a simple way to adjust trim. Between organizing the paddler sequence, adjusting the bow seat and distributing the equipment, we maintained fairly good trim.

Where it gets trickier is when there's a large weight differential between crewmembers. It's not that unreasonable to have a 100-pound weight differential between paddlers in a tandem crew (such as a 225-pound person and a 125-pound person). In these cases, seat adjustment may not provide enough movement to balance the boat. We saw a number of cases where tandem canoe teams located a large cooler close to the lighter partner to better trim the boat.

In the end, teams with substantial weight differentials may not have enough equipment and have to add ballast in order to maintain trim. While adding weight is not desirable, it still may be better than spending all that additional paddling energy to keep the boat on course. And, if for some reason you lose your partner, adding ballast becomes a real necessity.

So how do you know if your boat is trim? If you look closely at pictures of MR340 boats at the start or finish line, you'll notice some have horizontal 1-inch strips of colored tape on the bow and stern spaced an inch apart. They're placed on the boat to provide a simple trim indicator. If the visible rows on the bow equal the visible rows on the stern, you're boat is level. If one end is high, move weight towards that end. For our canoe, I took a slightly different route since I was concerned that our Ground Crew might not be able to see us sitting still in the water with all the commotion at the start and at the checkpoints. After some measuring, I found that our canoe's wooden cross bars were parallel with the bottom of the canoe. Using tie wraps, I strapped a small plastic carpenters level to the cross bar in front of my seat so I could quickly glance at it to see if we were running level. It turns out that I stopped looking at it after the third checkpoint since we always seemed to be trim. This consistency was mostly due to us not radically altering our weight distribution. We usually sat in the same spots and each person had their own food and water supply which further distributed the weight evenly. That said, Ellen, while in the stern, did mention a few times when she went to sit on the bottom to take a nap that there was water sloshing around. In thinking about it, I now realize that we might not have been as level as I first believed, since pooling water in the stern would indicate that our bow was riding high. What kind of difference it made is hard to tell, but no matter what method you use to track your trim, take a look at what the water[6] in the boat is doing to reconfirm your measurements.

I have been on the Missouri River when the wind whipped up strong enough to form white caps and actually blow our canoe upstream, so I know minimizing the wind's effect can be a big advantage. Here, the physics calculation is pretty simple: The taller the boat, the more impact from wind. So, in a race between a canoe and a kayak where head wind is a factor, the kayak will have the advantage because of its lower profile.

Canoeists sometimes add a spray skirt over the top of their canoe to keep out water in a white water river. Skirts can also be used to aerodynamically streamline the canoe and reduce wind resistance.

Now that we understand the physics behind boat design, let's take a look at the type of boats competing in the MR340 to determine which one is right for you.

Canoes

The basic canoe design has been around for thousands of years. Developed by the native peoples of North America, the first canoes were built by covering a wooden frame with birch bark or by hollowing out a felled log. Explorers and trappers took the native people's design one step further by expanding the size of these boats in order to carry large amounts of trade goods.

Then came Grumman. I suspect that everyone participating in the MR340 has, at one time or another, paddled a Grumman aluminum canoe. Developed near the end of World War II, Grumman canoes have been the choice of paddlers and outfitters everywhere because of their ruggedness and durability. But as I mentioned previously, that ruggedness comes at a price, namely more weight.

Companies such as Wenonah refined Grumman's approach by introducing lighter materials like Kevlar and graphite, and refining the hull shape for better efficiency in the water. But while Wenonah's designs may be more efficient and lighter than a Grumman's, they still have a large wetted surface due to their large cargo capacity and, as a result, have more frictional resistance than many kayaks. So why use a canoe for the MR340?

To answer that question, it's helpful to follow our boat decision process.

---

[6] **What's water doing in the boat? Just by virtue of switching from side to side, your paddle will drip water in the boat. Multiply that by four paddlers and it's easy over time to build up a small to medium pool of water that sloshes around the bottom of the boat. We used a large sponge to soak up this water and to also clean up mud we tracked in from the checkpoints. Besides rain and swamping, this is one more way that things get wet.**

For our team, there were a number of considerations: Space for four people and gear, our experience level and availability.

When I first signed us up, the plan was for Ellen and Christine to paddle in one boat, and Rob and I to paddle in another. The key assumption here was that Rob and I could keep up with Ellen and Christine (or vice versa) since we were only going to have a single Ground Crew to support both boats.

That plan changed when Rob got a full-time internship in May with no time off, and Claire decided she wanted to go as a paddler. I searched around for another paddler since I wasn't sure Claire and I could do it ourselves but didn't have much luck, so by mid-June (45 days before show time), I decided the smartest approach would be to have all four of us in the same boat.

Having that large of a crew considerably limited the number of options. While I did see outrigger boats available[7], I was concerned with our lack of experience with those types of boats and their limited space.

It might seem odd to talk about the need for space in a boat, but ours was driven by two factors; flexibility in paddling position and sleep.

I had just had back surgery for a ruptured disk that prior December, and while my recovery was uneventful, I had continual nightmares about something going wrong with my back during the race. My theory was, if I had a way to adjust my paddling position, I could minimize any problems, or if something happened, I would have the flexibility to figure out a different position where I could keep paddling. A canoe offered the best flexibility.

Our need to sleep in the boat was more a reflection of our race strategy. I had no illusions about our speed. I didn't think we were going to be able to sprint ahead, get way in front of the clock and sleep on shore. Instead, we would have to get ahead of the cut-off time by staying in the boat. That meant we had to find a way to sleep while paddling.

The good news about having four paddlers meant that we could very easily sleep two people at the same time. That was assuming, however, that we could figure out how to sleep on the boat, and for that, a canoe once again proved to be the best choice by offering plenty of space.

Canoes were readily available, too. While it's certainly desirable to have something fast, there are a number of other things you'll want to consider when attempting a race of this length and duration.

For us, as it will be for you, it's a combination of crew size, space and our experience level which drove us to selecting a canoe over a kayak or outrigger.

---

[7] **The Rivermiles Forum is a great place to look for rental or "For Sale" boats.**

Kayaks

Developed and used by the native peoples of the sub-arctic, kayaks differ from canoes by seating the paddler much lower in the water. Being closer to the water greatly impacts the angle in which you can paddle, so kayakers use double-bladed paddles as opposed to the single blade paddles used for canoes. Kayaks have a covered deck as opposed to the open bow of canoes and contain a skirted cockpit where paddlers sit. One big difference in the design of the kayak versus a canoe is the ability to recover quickly after flipping. While it might take 20 minutes to right a swamped canoe, experienced kayakers, by rotating their hips and using their paddle, can right the boat just as fast as it flipped, very helpful when you're in the surf or going down Class IV rapids.

Thirty years ago you would have been hard pressed to find someone using a kayak. Today, with stores like Dick's Sporting Goods and Cabela's offering a wide array of shapes and styles at reasonable prices, kayaks have overcome canoes as the preferred mode of water recreation.

Just as with canoes, kayak designs are constrained by the laws of physics. Longer kayaks have a higher theoretical hull speed but usually at the expense of turning ability. Wider kayaks are much more stable but at the expense of holding track. The kayaks sold by Dick's are designed wide for stability but are not good candidates for long races such as the MR340 due to their inefficiencies. Longer, narrower kayaks are fast and efficient due their low wetted surface area and their ability to hold track. The drawback as we know is their primary stability.

I was extremely jealous of MR340 kayakers due to their ease of paddling. But I constantly reminded myself that in order to paddle a kayak, it took a higher degree of technique than what we had to have with canoes. I'll bet you could give me any canoe out there and I could paddle it very well within five minutes. I could probably do that as well with any recreational kayaks sold by Cabela's. But there's no way I'd be able to do that with one of the long, narrow, efficient kayaks I saw used in the MR340.

So we're back to the choice of canoe or kayak. Both have pluses and minuses, but what makes the most sense for a first timer?

If I was a solo paddler, I would do everything in my power to use a kayak. While it may mean lots of training and instruction, the advantages in speed and efficiencies you get in a solo kayak versus a solo canoe are just too much to pass up.

If I was on a tandem team I'd be okay with either a canoe or kayak. A canoe gives you lots of flexibility during the race (like sleeping), whereas a kayak gives you efficiencies. Either is available for purchase or for rent.

Finally, if I had a team of three or more, I would have to choose the canoe. There are 3-person kayaks out there, but I don't think I've ever seen a 4-man. In addition, as you have those extra bodies, the logistics to support them on the river get more complicated, and having the storage and space capability of a canoe provides additional flexibility for the crew.

High Performance Racers

If you're so inclined, take a look at racing boats. There are many different types of racing boats, all designed to meet unique size, layout and weight specifications. Just as Indy 500 racecars have to meet specific race constraints in order to compete, there are canoe and kayak races that only allow a specific type of boat. Most of these races are governed by the International Canoe Federation (ICF) which has specified classes of canoes and kayaks. The designs are often referred to as C1 (solo canoe), C2 (tandem canoe), etc. for canoes, and K1 (solo kayak), K2 (tandem kayak), etc. for kayaks.

What you'll quickly realize about these designs is that they are optimized for much shorter duration races. Sprint races usually go up to 1000 meters, World Cup and World Championship distance races are usually less than 25 miles. Just because they aren't designed for something like the MR340 doesn't mean people don't try to use them there, but they spend lots of time thinking of ways to adapt them to a race 340 miles long.

While I'm all about finding a fast boat, using boats such as these requires an advanced skill set. It's one thing to have used a racing boat for years in shorter races and then want to use them to move up to the MR340. It's something else to select one of these for a race of this magnitude without much experience.

Home-Built/Experimental

In the 2009 MR340 DVD, one of the teams made its own canoe out of used plastic barrels. Team members spliced strips of these barrels together with rivets, and with a judicious amount of caulk they proceeded to build a river-worthy canoe that they paddled 340 miles. Later I heard the rest of the story. They donated the canoe at the end of the race and then bought two used bicycles which they used to pedal home.

During our race in 2012, a team consisting of four men built and paddled their own sort of catamaran thingy (without the sail of course). It was an especially interesting design in that they built it so all four could paddle it, except that the way they were situated in the boat meant they couldn't switch sides paddling without physically switching places in the boat. We chatted with them a little right after the start and caught up with them again at Jefferson City.

These two teams are a good illustration of good old American ingenuity and of how it's possible to finish in something other than "store bought." What a contrast it is to compare their approach with ours. While we went for the proven approach, they were ready and willing to push the envelope and give something different a try. While the engineer (and father) in me may never let me be that brave, it was both humbling and an honor to be in a race that contained such true adventurers.

Paddles

Fifty thousand – that's how many strokes each of us paddled over the course of the race[8]. That's a huge number, especially when you realize that your paddle is directly tied to each and every one of those strokes.

My experience with canoe paddles started way back at Boy Scout camp. There we were issued a heavy wooden paddle whose only helpful attribute besides moving the canoe was that it floated after you swamped. Later, as I started paddling the Ozark streams of mid-Missouri, I used paddles with aluminum shafts and plastic blades. I never really considered anything else until my son and I went on a 42-mile trip down the Meramec River near St. Louis. We paddled with Mike Claypool and his sons, who had outfitted themselves with beautiful, lightweight, bent-shaft paddles from Bending Branches. But pretty's not necessarily functional, so I didn't pay much attention to them until Mike offered to switch paddles 30 miles into the float.

Then I saw the light, or at least felt it.

Besides being beautiful, Mike's paddles were incredibly lightweight compared to the wooden ones we had been using. The difference would have been noticeable at the start, but 30 miles in, the weight difference was huge. I mentioned earlier how every pound of weight makes a difference, but here's a case where every ounce makes a difference. Let's compare: A typical economy wooden paddle from Cabela's ($18) might weigh more than 35 ounces; an aluminum economy paddle from Campmor ($20) might weight around 30 ounces; and a Whiskey Jack "Jill" Ultralight Wood Laminate Paddle from Campmor ($139) weighs in at a mere 15 ounces.

As you can tell from the pricing, the less weight, the higher the cost. As you've already detected through my heavy use of the word "Walmart" throughout this book, I don't spend money when I don't have to, but this is one of the few areas where you can buy your way into substantial efficiencies. The even better news is you only have to get one per paddler so you can use a heavier, inexpensive one as the spare. But before deciding what to do, let's talk about what to look for in paddles in addition to weight.

I'm not going to cover how to measure yourself for a proper paddle fit. I've found that almost every paddle manufacturer has its own methodology for fitting it's paddles. When I bought paddles, I went to my preferred

---

[8] 60 hours on the river x 50% of the time paddling x 29 paddles per minute

manufacturer's site, figured out what measurements to take, measured all of us, and then went online and ordered. It isn't very hard to do, so take the time to do it according to the manufacturer's recommendation.

Here's the crew with our beautiful Whiskeyjack paddles showing the different lengths and blade sizes. Also notice the reflective tape around the lower part of the shaft. It's one more way to provide visibility to others while we paddled.

Blade shapes on paddles for canoes come in both wide and narrow. Wide is good for short bursts of paddling where you need to catch lots of water for power. Narrower blades don't catch as much water, which means they're less fatiguing when paddling some 50,000 strokes over the course of four days. Keeping that in mind, we opted to get narrow paddles for Claire and me, and wider paddles for Christine (more power) and Ellen (since she was going to be in the stern steering and a wider blade made it easier). We also figured that Claire and I could switch off paddles with them if someone needed a change of pace, although what we ended up doing was always keeping Ellen's paddle in the stern, so whoever was there got the wider paddle.

Canoe paddle handles come in two styles: T-Grip and Palm Grip. T-Grips allow you to grip the paddle tighter and are used more for whitewater paddling where there's rough water trying to twist your paddle about. The Palm Grip is a more relaxed grip and is much more comfortable when you're putting in lots of miles like the MR340.

Canoe paddle shafts can be straight, bent or crankshaft. Most everyone canoeing has used a straight shaft; it's by far the most common (and usually the cheapest) type of paddle on the market. As you move up in price, you'll start to see bent and crankshaft since they're typically marketed to a higher-end user. A bent paddle is one where the blade itself is bent at an angle. A crankshaft paddle looks like the letter "Z" lying on its side. The handle of the shaft is shifted forward relative to the blade. Why the funky shapes? For this explanation we'll turn not to physics but to geometry.

Think about where you obtain the most power from your paddle. That occurs when the paddle is fully perpendicular in the water, pushing the water back parallel to the boat. It doesn't occur at the beginning of a stroke since the paddle usually enters the water at an angle, meaning you're actually pushing some of the water down and you and your canoe up instead of forward. It also doesn't occur at the end of the stroke when instead of pushing the water down, you're pulling the water slightly up. Right where the blade is perpendicular to the water and parallel to the boat is the optimum spot for the paddle to propel your canoe forward.

Those reading ahead in the geometry book will quickly point out that no matter how you angle the paddle, there will still be points along your stroke path that won't be in the optimum position in the water, so why bother? Turns out bent and crankshaft paddles aren't designed to address paddle entry and exit angles. They're instead designed to locate the paddle perpendicular in the water at the exact place where your arms and body are positioned for the most power. It's hard to imagine a 12-degree bend making a difference, but if you have access to both a straight and a bent paddle, sit in a chair with the straight paddle and see where the paddle blade is facing when you think your arms are positioned for maximum power. Now try it with a bent shaft paddle. What you'll notice is that the bent paddle will be closer to perpendicular at your time of peak power position, whereas the straight paddle will have already started to come up out of the water.

So if bent and crankshaft paddles are so much more efficient, why would anyone use straight (besides cost)? The answer lies in how you're going to use them. Just with boats, paddles are optimized for events like long duration paddling or whitewater canoeing. While I would absolutely use a bent shaft for distance canoeing like the MR340, I would opt for a straight paddle when I float an Ozark stream, primarily because doing quick steering corrections to avoid rocks is much harder with a bent shaft than with a straight shaft.

Just as with canoe paddles, Kayak paddle blades vary in width. Wider blades will give you more "bite" but will be more fatiguing over a longer distance. Narrower blades are more efficient for longer distances, but require extra strokes to get up to speed.

Paddle weight is the next consideration. When I think lightweight I usually think of Kevlar or graphite, but in the case of paddles, you can get some very lightweight paddles made of wood (typically red and/or white cedar) overlaid with epoxied fiberglass. During my search I was less focused on construction material and more focused on where the price points were. I found there were three price segments for paddles: $30 or less for heavy duty wooden and aluminum, $100 to $140 for lightweight wooden or combination graphite/wooden, and more than $180 for graphite. Kayak paddles may be built from aluminum or graphite and, just as with canoe paddles, increase in price relative to their lighter weight.

If you want to start a fight at the Monday night safety meeting, go ahead and yell out "My XXXX paddle is the best paddle ever made," and watch how many people come over to argue. I never really knew until planning for the MR340 that some people own five or more paddles, every one of them optimized for different purposes. You won't need five paddles in the MR340; you'll just need the right one to get you to St. Charles. But while all I needed was seven miles with Mike's paddle to make my decision, you may want to do some testing before you pick the one you want.

But where can you test paddles? In St. Louis, besides the St. Louis Adventure Club, there's the St. Louis Canoe and Kayak Club. Look around for clubs such as these or outdoor stores like The Alpine Shop who put on paddling clinics and see when they're going to hit the water. I guarantee you all you have to do is say "MR340" and you'll have thirty people offering boats and paddles to test as well as lots of advice. The other advantage about groups like these is there's always somebody who selling something. A good paddle is going to cost between $100 and $140 new, so you might be able to pick up one slightly used for much less.

Because I struggled with choosing a canoe or a kayak, I got a very late start with lining up paddles. While I really enjoyed the feel of Mike's Bending Branches Sunburst paddle, I absolutely fell in love when I borrowed Josh Pennington's Whiskeyjack paddle. Light and comfortable, the Whiskeyjack series of paddles can be bought through Campmor in all the sizes we needed. To call them paddles doesn't do them justice. They are wonderful works of art that look spectacular. But buying three paddles (I borrowed the fourth) was the single most expensive investment we made ($450). I wrestled with the cost but finally convinced myself that the weight reduction was worth the investment. Having successfully completed the race, I can say with certainty that having something this light helped tremendously in getting us to the finish line.

Which is not to say all is lost if you can't swing purchasing these. Look for used paddles, and if that doesn't work, try renting. I believe a lightweight paddle is the single most important (and expensive) piece of gear you'll get for the MR340.

But if you're trying to convince your significant other about why you want to purchase expensive paddles, you're more than welcome to use my story. When I was 14, I went with my Boy Scout troop to the Boundary Waters outside of Ely, Minnesota, where we had an incredible time. About halfway through our trip my paddle broke, proving why you need to keep a spare. I ended up carrying that broken paddle back from the Boundary Waters where it moved with me from closet to closet, house to house, always there to remind me of my adventure. Since having that memento gave me such good memories, I thought it would be fun to give my daughters the same present. So there in my basement sit three beautiful, slightly used wooden canoe paddles that will someday have the MR340 logo embossed on them, available to be mounted on their trophy wall. Ready and raring for the next race.

MR340 Required Equipment

The MR340 rules require you to carry the following equipment aboard your boat during the race:

Personal Floatation Devices

PDFs are designed to assist in the floatation of the wearer and must be worn at all times. They're classified into five different category types by the United States Coast Guard (USCG) based on their application and the amount of buoyancy they provide.

Notice that the amount of buoyancy they provide isn't equal to the weight of the wearer but instead takes advantage of the body's natural floatation and provides enough extra buoyancy to keep the wearer's head out of the water. The buoyancy provided may exceed 22 pounds for a Type 1 PFD to 15.5 pounds for Type II and III.

Type I - Offshore Lifejacket – Designed for extended survival in open water. Provides 22 pounds of buoyancy.

Type II - Near Shore Buoyant Vest – Designed for calm inland water with many having the ability to turn an unconscious person face up in the water.

Type III - Flotation Aid – Making up the largest category of PFDs at places like Cabela's, Bass Pro or Walmart, the Type IIIs are designed for water sports and boating activities in calm waters. Unlike the Type I & II, they are usually not designed to turn over an unconscious person, but as a result may be lighter and more comfortable with a wider variety of shapes and sizes.

Type III can also include inflatable or "on-demand" PFDs. This type of PFD features a smaller, more comfortable profile since it inflates via a CO_2 cartridge only when it's in the water.

Type IV - Throwable Device – Includes rings and seat cushions which are not designed to be worn but instead be used in emergencies.

Type V - Special Use Device – Includes working vests and deck suits wore by boat crews.

Whether you use a Type I, II or III PFD, all provide flotation safety and will make you compliant to the race rules. These could include an $18 one from Walmart up to a $130 one from REI. The challenge isn't finding one that'll help you float; it's finding one that won't rub you raw after four days of paddling.

We considered three things when selecting our PFDs: Adjustability, pockets and cooling. Cheaper PFDs may only have one zipper, no pockets and no ability to adjust the snugness. We looked for PFDs that not only had adjustable straps around the torso but also had adjustable straps over the shoulder. This is especially important if you're a woman since as far as I can tell, all PFD designers are male.

The ability to adjust and readjust your PFD is a critical advantage over a four-day race. Places on your body that were fine on Day 1 may be rubbing on Day 3. Adjustments also help you keep on the PFD. We saw a number of times where a paddler's PFD was unbuckled, most likely due to rubbing or heat. Besides being against the rules, think of our 40-second encounter with Captain Ahab. We barely had time to get out of the way, much less spend time buckling up our PFDs. PFDs only help when they're on and buckled. You'll have enough problems if you go swimming rather than to have to worry about a PFD that's yanked over your head because it wasn't secure.

Besides adjustments, we also looked for PFDs that helped keep us cool. PFDs with mesh (or nothing at all) as opposed to solid material around the sides and shoulders are going to allow air to circulate. Your PFD will be taking full sun, and mesh will allow your body to breathe better. Look also at the edging. Many of the mesh PFDs we looked at also had softer material around the neck area; cheaper solid material ones usually didn't and will rub you ragged.

Another consideration with respect to cooling was to look for PFDs in lighter colors. Lighter colors reflect sunlight better than darker colors.

Our final consideration was pockets where we could store a snack bar, small flashlight, whistle and Mylar reflective blanket. Should you go swimming, it's these things you'll want with you as you sit on the shore signaling for help.

We purchased Cabela's Full Motion Type III PFDs on sale ($45). Designed for kayakers (meaning that they're designed to be shorter than traditional boating PFDs), they were adjustable and had pockets. Whereas some PFDs we looked at had mesh, these didn't have any material at all joining the floatation pieces, just straps. The only drawback to these was they were made in dark colors. I understand from a standpoint of keeping them clean as to why they would be darker not lighter, but darker PFDs will heat up in the sun more than lighter ones. They also came in a number of different sizes, so it's worthwhile to try on a number of them just to make sure you get the best fit. PFDs can get pricey, but in my opinion it ranked near the top as best investment for the money. It's the one thing that you'll wear and won't be able to change your whole time on the water, so paying $25 more so something won't rub your skin off is worthwhile.

Whistle

Used for signaling, we bought one for each of us (Walmart, $2 each). Whatever you get, make sure it has a lanyard so you can tie it to your PFD. If you end up going swimming, you'll want the whistle with you, not in the boat or worse yet at the bottom of the river.

Flashlight

Oddly enough, solving the flashlight puzzle ended up taking the most effort of everything I did to prepare. But based on that experience I'll try to simplify the approach.

You'll need waterproof flashlights for three different purposes: To find stuff like equipment, food, drinks and clothes in the boat; to find buoys, channel markers and mileage markers; and to signal other boats in case of an emergency. Unfortunately, one flashlight doesn't necessarily fit the bill for all these applications, so we ended up bringing three types of flashlights along with us.

Here we are taking off from Jefferson City under the watchful supervision of Linda. By the time we left Jefferson City, we were in a more relaxed state. Note the girls in shorts and no hats. The wing dike in the background caused a strong backward current on the back side of the dike, surprising many paddlers arriving from Katfish Katy's as they cut across to the landing area.

151

You can't really discuss flashlights without discussing the full moon. On one of the first outings I went on with my son's Cub Scout den, we decided to go on a night hike, and of course everyone had to bring their newly bought flashlight. The problem was, because of the full moon, we didn't need flashlights at all. As long as you kept the flashlight off, your eyes adjusted extremely well to the moonlight, and navigating the trail was very easy.

Each year the MR340 is scheduled around the full moon, so as long as you don't have cloud cover, you're almost guaranteed a very bright night. Note, however, that the moonrise doesn't necessarily coincide with sunset and sunrise, so it's possible you will be in the dark for some portion of the race (or all of it depending on the cloud cover). But when the moon's up, it's bright.

Using a single, very bright flashlight to find something in the boat was a concern for two reasons. First, we would have had to pass it back and forth increasing the chance that we'd drop and break it. Secondly, a big bright flashlight would have ruined everyone's night vision. So we instead opted to have everyone carry a small MagLite solitaire pen flashlight (Walmart, $7) although any small waterproof key-chain light would do. We made sure they had a lanyard, which we tied to an extractable plastic clip-on key reel (Walmart, $3). We then attached the key reel to each of our PFDs. That way everyone always had access to one (especially if we went swimming), and we didn't have to worry about unclipping and re-clipping. It was also out of the way until we needed it.

Just a quick thought about batteries: When selecting electronic equipment to bring, think about what size batteries they use. In a perfect world, every piece of equipment you bring would use the same size battery, so that the spares you bring could be used in multiple pieces of equipment.

The reality is it's hard to get that lucky, so think "redundancy" and "battery life" instead. Take our pen lights. They used one "AAA" battery, which kept the flashlight small, but unfortunately no other electronics in the boat used that size. But that said, we decided not to bring any spares of that size for two reasons. First, since these pen lights are LEDs instead of incandescent, they have an extremely long battery life (more than 100 hours), so we literally could have turned them on at the start of the race and they would have stayed on past the time we arrived in St. Charles. Secondly, since each of us had one, we could always pass one back and forth if someone's died.

LED flashlights put out much more light than incandescent and use way less power. So why are they still selling incandescent flashlights? Got me, but I can tell you manufacturers make it very confusing if you're not looking. For example they say "100 ft" in big letters when the flashlight right next to it will say "100 lumens". What's the difference? One hundred feet isn't very far away, and if it's an incandescent, it may not last a night on one set of batteries. If it's a 100 lumen LED flashlight, you may be able to see 200 meters (600 feet) and one set of batteries will last you the whole week.

Our second flashlight was a Dorcy waterproof, lightweight, 130 lumen LED light (Campmor, $24) we kept in the boat at all times. Using 4 AA batteries, it too had a very long life when compared with incandescent and was relatively light. I had hoped to use this as the primary flashlight for buoys and markers but found that while it put out 130 lumens, it was not focusable, meaning that it put out a halo of light, not a focused beam. It worked well for shorter, wider illumination as opposed to seeing things at a distance.

Because of the limits of the Dorcy flashlight, we also used a waterproof, focusable 136 Lumen LED MagLite (Lowe's, $57). While expensive and very heavy (three C batteries), this flashlight provided a focusable beam with which we could spot buoys, mile markers and navigation signs from a long way away. Because it was so heavy, we packed this flashlight in our night bag, which the Ground Crew gave us in the evening, and took out of the boat the next morning.

While probably overkill, having two big flashlights enabled both me and Christine to work in tandem. She would use the MagLite to spot things on the river most of the time, where I would use the Dorcy flashlight for the times she was resting. In addition to not carrying extra batteries, having two also provided redundancies in case we lost or broke one.

Reflective blanket

Each of us a Mylar reflective blanket (Walmart, $3) in the pocket of our PFD. Carried by hikers, these blankets are very lightweight, and when wrapped around you, reflect your body heat to keep you warm. While adequate for an individual, these blankets aren't really rugged enough to use as a canopy or tarp. Being a good Boy Scout, at the start of the race I packed rain jackets for each of the crew. By the end of the first day, with the heat peaking at 104 degrees and no rain in sight for the next few days, I ditched the rain jackets with the intent on using the reflective blankets. Had rain been in the forecast, I don't think I would have solely counted on the reflective blankets, but faced with little or no chance of rain, these blankets are a good alternative to rain gear.

Enough food/water to make it to the next checkpoint

We discussed hydration and food in great detail in earlier chapters, but be aware that having enough food and water to make it to the next checkpoint isn't just a good idea; it's required by the race rules.

Cell phone in waterproof case and spare charged battery

Why a cell phone when you're out in the middle of nowhere? While it may seem like you're in the wilderness, there were very few times we couldn't get a Verizon cell phone signal (this will vary depending on the carrier). Besides the primary benefit of calling for help in an emergency, a cell phone also allows you to check the weather and your location and contact your Ground Crew.

With our team having four cell phones, we opted for keeping two in the boat as opposed to just having one with extra batteries. We kept the one we used in a Ziploc bag stored in a compression bag. The backup we turned off and stored in a waterproof speaker (more on that later) up front with Christine. Cell phones that can't get a signal draw lots of power, so we kept at least one off so both didn't discharge at the same time.

The Ground Crew used one and kept the remaining one charging in the car using a DC to 120 VAC Power Inverter (Walmart, $30 for a 600-watt model[9]). When they met us at a checkpoint, I'd give the one I used to the Ground Crew, move the one from Christine back to me, and the one the Ground Crew charged to Christine. This system worked well except for trying to keep track of which phone number to call the Ground Crew on since we kept moving phones around (nothing like calling yourself).

One thing we didn't realize is just how damp everything gets on the boat. I thought having the cell phone in the plastic bag would keep it dry, but after a while you could see the condensation in both the Ziploc and the compression bag. And that's with no rain. Get a waterproof cell phone cover if you can afford it. Cell phones are fairly robust, but I'm not sure the way we did it would have worked in a downpour.

Virtual Monitoring if unsupported

If you're paddling without the support of a Ground Crew, you'll need to have a "virtual" Ground Crew that is monitoring you from home by some means. Monitoring may be by cell phone or by Spot Tracker (GPS devices that report your location via satellite). The intent is to make sure your virtual Ground Crew knows that you made it to a check point, your plans for the next stretch and when they should hear from you again.

Spot Trackers have really come on the outdoors scene in the past few years. Consisting of a GPS tracker that reports its position to a web site via a satellite connection, Spot Trackers are a perfect way to let your Ground Crew and those fans back home know where you are on the river. There's a

---

[9] **If all you're going to do is recharge phones, a power inverter that just has a USB connection would work. We brought one that had both 120 VAC outlets as well as USB ports. They're not that much more expensive and give you the capability to run laptops, xboxes and other household electrical equipment from the car.**

number of different versions that can either be purchased or rented.

For unsupported paddlers, Spot Trackers are required to provide a way for Scott and his staff to keep tabs on those racers. For the rest of us with Ground Crews, it's more for convenience.

While we rented a Spot Tracker (look at the Rivermiles Forum for rental information, $33) for the race, we didn't have much luck with it. First, we didn't bother to tell anyone we had a tracker (whoops), so no one knew they could watch our progress, and secondly, the Spot Tracker system we used that year required a Flash Plug-in, which thanks to Apple doesn't work on the iPad and iPhones our Ground Crew used during the race. (Note that this can change depending on what Spot Tracking system is used. If you're interested in getting a Spot Tracker for the race and you're an Apple product user, make sure you ask about compatibility.)

There are alternatives. Many cell phones have "Phones Around Me" apps which your Ground Crew and fans can use to track your progress. But remember that these apps assume you're within range of a cell tower, which may not always be the case depending on your provider.

While Spot Trackers can also be helpful in estimating arrival times to your Ground Crew, we found there was very little variation in our speed over the course of the race (we varied from 5.8 to 6.2 mph). Because of that consistency, we were fairly confident at one checkpoint when we'd be hitting the next one. We also got into the habit of calling six miles out (one hour away), just to give the Ground Crew a heads up that we were close. For those reasons I wouldn't consider having a Spot Tracker a necessity (unless you're paddling unsupported), although it's a cool way to keep people at home up to date (given that you tell them).

10 Feet of Rope.

The 10 feet of rope specified in the rules is to assist in towing. And while helpful, 10 feet of rope isn't going to do much more than that. For our boat, we tied 10 feet of rope to the bow (front of the boat) and tied the other end in a throw knot (a knot designed to allow quick unraveling of the rope). We also added a second 100-foot rope with one end tied to the stern (rear of the boat) and the other end tied to a Type IV throwable device (better known as a seat cushion). If someone fell out of the boat, it was Ellen's job in the stern to throw out the seat cushion. It could also be used for other paddlers needing assistance.

Full navigation lighting.

Full navigation lighting consists of a red and green light on the bow (called a sidelight), and a white sternlight on the stern. The intent of the navigation lighting is twofold. First, it allows your boat to be seen by other boats, and secondly, it enables other boats to tell which way your boat is moving relative to them.

Let's discuss the boat movement first. Since green is always on the boat's right (or starboard) side, if you see a boat in front of you and only see their green light; that means that they're moving from left to right across your bow. Likewise, if you see their red light (on their left, or port side[10]), that means they're moving across your bow in the opposite way.

Where you need to get concerned is when you see both their red and green lights since that means they're coming toward you. When that happens, shine your flashlight along the side of your boat to let them know you're there.

Here we are landing at the finish in St. Charles. It's a good picture to show how our bow and stern lights were mounted. Note how the bow light faces forward and the stern light is elevated and tilted back to keep the light out of the boat. Also note the split section of swimming noodle at the bow to cushion Christine's leg from the canoe. These types of boat are very narrow in front for efficiency, which doesn't give the paddler much room compared to the stern positions.

---

[10] Port and Left both have four letters. That's the only way I can remember that port is left and therefore starboard is right.

Seeing just sternlights is a good thing. The most beautiful sights you'll see besides the finish line is a stream of white lights in front of you at 3 a.m., showing you the way to St. Charles.

So now that we know how navigation lights are used, let's talk about being seen. Navigation lights aren't just a MR340 requirement; they're mandated by the USCG for inland waterway vessels. USCG rules[11] specify that for boats less that 12 meters in length (better known as us), the sidelight must be visible one mile away and the sternlight, two miles away.

We saw all kinds of navigation lights used during the race. They ranged from standard navigation lights borrowed from speed boats to tea lights and glow sticks. Most would say theirs were adequate since no one got run over, but from a safety standpoint, some were certainly more robust than others. Here are things to consider when you're trying to be seen at night:

Intensity –USCG regulations specify the luminous light range for navigation in a unit called candelas. Candelas is a measurement of light intensity in a specific direction as opposed to lumens which measures the total amount of light that is emitted. Another way to think about it is reading a book using a candle. It might be hard to read just using a lit candle since the candle's light radiates in all directions (lumens). If you're able to focus that light in one specific area, the lumens didn't increase (it's still one candle measured in lumens), but the intensity (candelas) did increase.

Why do you care? Because you'll want to make sure your navigation lighting is compliant, and many times lights are rated in lumens, not candelas. Lucky for us there's a quick approximation we can use to roughly convert lumens to candelas (1 candelas = 12.57 lumens).

For your sidelight to be visible at one mile, it's 0.9 candelas (11.2 lumens); for the sternlight visibility at two miles, it's 4.3 candelas (54 lumens). Do you get arrested if your light provide more than required? Nope, the USCG only specifies a minimum intensity. But over-sizing the lights means additional weight you'd just as soon avoid.

A quick way to see if your navigation lights meet USCG requirements is to check the light bulb wattage. As a rule of thumb, 2-watt flashlight bulb or a ½-watt LED bulb will emit approximately 20 lumens. The sidelight we used contained a 2.38-watt light bulb which meant it provided more than 20 lumens of light (more than enough for the sidelight).

Not sure what the bulb wattage is? Look up the bulb number at Radio Shack (www.radioshack.com) or Batteries Plus (www.batteriesplus.com), and then look under specifications for the wattage. If you're really lucky the specifications   might even specify candelas (usually identified as "candle

[11] United States Coast Guard NAVIGATION RULES INTERNATIONAL—INLAND NAVIGATION, COMDTINST M16672.2D

power").

Still confused? Buy a kit from a company that's already done the math. Walmart sells an Attwood Portable Navigation Light Kit ($30) which includes both the sidelight and sternlight.

Glow sticks are another option. Just make sure they're rated high enough in intensity. Realize also that the lumen rating is around the whole glow stick, so you'd be wise to get a higher lumen rating since one side will be exposed and the other side will be against the boat.

Mounting – As with intensity, the USGC also specifies where the navigation lighting is mounted, and what angles they need to be visible. The sidelight is mounted in the bow of the boat, with the green light on the starboard side and red on the port, and both should be visible within a 135-degree arc of the bow. The sternlight should be mounted at the stern of the boat and be visible within a 135-degree arc over the horizon. This sounds simple enough until you realize the basic problem with almost all the boats entered in the MR340 is that they weren't designed for navigation lights.

Because each boat is different, there's no "one way" to mount your navigation lights. But there are five key considerations when figuring out how to mount your lights:

1. *Make them secure:* However you mount them, navigation lights need to be able to survive rain, wind and swamping. Since you're probably not going to be drilling holes in your rented boat, there's two ways to affix the lights on your boat. Tie them down using string/rope/tie wraps/bungee cords, or use Velcro strips. For the bow, our sidelight was mounted to a board which was designed to slide into the bow and be retained by a bungee cord. If you decide to use Velcro, you might want to put duct tape on first, then tape the Velcro over the duct tape. The duct tape will adhere better to the boat and comes off easier than the Velcro. However you mount them, hit/wiggle/rock it to make sure it's secure and that it'll take a dunking. If not, add more tape. We also brought with us a small roll of duct tape just in case we needed to make any adjustments along the way. You'll see some just plain ugly mountings with duct tape and straps all over the place. But it's not about being pretty, it's about being secure.

2. *Limit glare:* The point of having navigation lights is to let others know where you are, not to let yourself know. Seems silly, but I was amazed at how many paddlers stared into their own navigation lights instead of mounting them in a way where the lights shined away from them and into other boating traffic. This is especially true for the sternlight. Because it's both bright and white, if mounted too low on the boat, it'll cause a halo of light around your boat and wreck your night vision. Mounting your sternlight on a 3-4 foot pole that tilts away from the boat limits the amount of light you'll have to deal with while at the same time improves visibility to others. For the sidelights, try and mount them not on the top of the boat's

bow but on the side. You might also consider placing something over the top of them to further minimize glare. The point is for them to be visible outward, not upward to you. Our sternlight consisted of a Sylvania DOTS LED Tap Light Bulb (Walmart, $7) placed in a 16 oz. clear plastic peanut butter jar whose lid was attached to a 1-inch diameter, 4-foot-long PVC pipe which we then tied to our stern and duct taped to the bottom of the canoe. It was tilted back slightly so very little light spilled into the canoe, but it could be seen very well from a distance.

3. *Make them weatherproof:* It goes without saying that the lights need to be waterproof. But what you also must consider is that the mounting needs to be waterproof/sun proof/heatproof as well. If you're using tape or Velcro, don't skimp with lightweight stuff. Your mountings have to last through the heat of the day and dampness of the night, all along getting bumped and doused.

4. *Make them accessible:* Usually, accessing navigation lights isn't that a big deal. When you pull out of a checkpoint close to dark, just make sure you turn them on while standing on shore. If you have LED navigation lights, your mission's accomplished. They'll probably last from then to St. Charles. But we did see some which needed hourly help. Walmart has glow sticks ($5) in red and green which make perfect sidelights. The only problem is they only stay on one hour, then turn off. You have to re-click the button to turn them back on. While this works great for kids who forget to turn things off, it's a real problem if they're mounted where you can't reach on the bow of your 18-foot kayak. A canoe wouldn't be that big of a problem (besides the hassle of every hour hitting the button), but if you're in a kayak, make sure you pick something that doesn't require that kind of effort (or make sure you're near people who can help).

5. *Remember duration:* Be aware of your light's duration. As we already discussed, many LED lights have more than 100 hours of operation on one set of batteries, enabling you to turn them on at the start and forget about them. Incandescent will chew up batteries much faster, so you and your Ground Crew will need to remember to turn them off in the morning and be ready with another set of batteries the next night.

Reflective Tape on your Boat

Most production boats have this, but as they say, more never hurts. We bought strips of Hillman Group 2-inch x 2-foot Safety Tape (Lowe's, $3 per strip) and taped strips of it all around the outside of our boat. We also wrapped reflective tape around the lower part of our paddles. You may also consider taping some to your PFD. While I thought about bringing running gear that has reflective material sewn in, but it was just too hard to make sure we would wear that one specific thing at night. Your PFD is the one thing you'll have on night and day, so anything you can add that reflects will help in case of an emergency.

Spare paddle

You should only need to use an extra paddle if your main paddle breaks or if you somehow lose it, so the spare paddle doesn't have to be anything more than functional. Multi-person boats need only one per boat. Make sure you tie it down. You don't want to be reaching for the spare after you go swimming only to find out it went swimming, too.

Four-Digit Boat Number

Rules require your 4-digit boat number to be affixed to both sides of the boat in reflective 3" mailbox or motorboat numbers (Lowe's, $2.75 each). There is some serious glue on these numbers, so place duct tape on the boat where you want to put the numbers, and then stick the numbers on the duct tape. This will make removal easier and prevent damage to the boat.

Safety extras we added

Besides what's specified in the rules, we also added the following safety items:

First Aid Kit – We assembled our own lightweight first aid kit that we placed in a transparent, waterproof compression bag. You can absolutely buy these separately, but it's much easier to buy a first aid kit (Walmart) for the Ground Crew and take the pieces you need from it for the boat. Our boat first aid kit consisted of the following:

- 5-10 small waterproof bandages
- Four small round waterproof bandages (For men: Apply over nipples to prevent chafing. The dreaded chafing nipple effect is common occurrence for male long distance runners. Depending on what shirt you wear it might be a problem for this race.)
- Small roll of duct tape (Unroll 10 feet from a larger roll instead of buying something small)
  - Small roll of waterproof first aid tape
  - One roll of Rolaids
  - Small bottle of 30 SPF sunscreen
  - Bottle of Tylenol
  - Small bottle of Pepto Bismal
  - Anti-diarrheal caplets (Walgreens, $5)
  - Chapstick with SPF15 for each person
  - Band-Aid Advanced Healing Blister Cushions (Walgreens, $6)
  - Handi-wipes
  - Body Glide Anti-Chafe Balm (Sports Authority, $10)
  - Extra batteries (We bought Lithium. Very expensive, but we wanted to

make sure they were heavy duty enough to last.)

- Moleskin with small scissors or knife to cut patches
- Handkerchiefs

There are a few items that may not be familiar. Besides having Pepto Bismal to calm the stomach, we also brought anti-diarrheal medicine. Having diarrhea's a bad day both from a hydration and a time-stopped perspective. Having those tablets handy could get you to the next checkpoint.

Our hands held up remarkably well considering they were in constant use for four days. Most of us used a combination of waterproof first aid tape and Band-Aid Advanced Healing Blister Cushions. Ellen's left hand on far right of pictures shows her use of three blister cushions. They seemed to have held up better than everyone else's tape.

Blister cushions are truly a miracle of modern medical technology. Since my childhood scouting days I've used moleskin (a fuzzy flexible piece of cloth with adhesive on the back) to tape over emerging blisters on my hands and feet. Initially for the race we brought waterproof tape and moleskin, but Linda saw someone using these blister cushions at one of the checkpoints and immediately got us a couple of boxes. Oftentimes when you put moleskin on your hands, it'll prevent blisters from one spot but will cause rubbing somewhere else, so it becomes a big game of blister "Whack-A-Mole." The blister cushions are designed to protect the emerging blister, plus it's padded so the rubbing isn't transferred to another spot. By the end of the race, besides being swollen, our hands were in pretty good shape due to these cushions[12].

Body Glide Anti-Chafe Balm is something many runners use on their feet to prevent blisters. We used it for anywhere we started to feel rubbing (under the arms, on the butt). The key to using this and the blister cushions is to start sooner rather than later. Something slightly rubbing outside of Lexington will be horrific by Jefferson City, so spend a few minutes applying a fix or making an equipment adjustment before it gets to be a real problem.

Unless you're going without a Ground Crew, remember that you don't have to bring enough first aid supplies for the whole trip; you only have to bring enough supplies to last until the next checkpoint. Also make sure both you and your Ground Crew are on the lookout for helpful items other teams may be using.

Bailer - If you flip, the immediate challenge will be to right the boat, then get the water out. There are two approaches. One is a kayak bilge pump (REI, $35). With a kayak's confined opening, being able to use a small hand-held pump while you're either in the kayak or out is helpful.

For us in a canoe, we cut the bottom off of a 1-gallon washer fluid bottle (leave the screw lid on) and tied it by a sting to somewhere on the boat so it didn't go floating. We brought along two, and kept one in front and one in back. Although we never had to use them to bail, we did use them for pee cups.

Tie-Downs - All your equipment should be tied to the boat in some way. Larger items like coolers should be tied tight enough so they wouldn't come out if you flip, since once they're out they can be very hard to get back in without getting to shore. The remaining items (compression bag, maps, seat cushions, etc.) can be tied loosely so they don't float too far away if you go swimming. If everything's connected with the boat, you'll be able to focus on righting the boat and not swimming madly around gathering equipment as it floats away.

For our coolers and water jugs, we installed locking ladder style buckles (Cabela's, $3 each) with 1-inch plastic straps. That way we could easily latch them around the seat and quickly remove them for resupply by the Ground Crew.

---

[12] I still laugh thinking about Walgreens and those blister cushions. They probably sell a box a week, and then all of a sudden within the span of 36 hours one summer week, they probably sold out for all of mid-Missouri. I'll bet they're still scratching their heads about what happened.

Other Equipment to Consider

As part of my approach to "accumulated advantages," we brought with us a number of other pieces of equipment that you may want to consider. While not essential, these pieces provide additional comfort which goes a long way in making 80-plus hours of paddling bearable.

Music – In 2009, we stood on top of Mount Elbert, the highest mountain in Colorado, admiring the spectacular scenery and talking among ourselves about the hike up, when along walks a 20-something guy with ear buds on. He had his music cranked loud enough where I could hear some of the THUMPA THUMPA as he walked by and I thought, "For gosh sakes, you couldn't turn off your music for two minutes to listen to what nature is all about at 14,000 feet?" My thoughts pretty much sum up my attitude about music and the outdoors in general. I can listen to AC/DC on the way to work. Why would I invite them along with me on a hike when there's nature to listen to instead?

Then I paddled for 77 hours…

To say that music saved us doesn't really capture its value. To say we wouldn't have made it would be more accurate. Traveling 340 miles takes an incredibly long time, and having music to help pass the time and keep you motivated was so unbelievably worthwhile. Looking through the Rivermiles Forum, I found a number of paddlers who made their own waterproof version of a sound system, but I was worried about how to mount one and the potential for getting our phone wet while using a home built system. While using ear buds was a possibility, I can't recommend them since you might not hear the boat or barge coming in behind you.

I opted instead for an Eco Extreme waterproof speaker case made by Grace Digital (Amazon, $35). You place your phone or iPod into a waterproof enclosure, plug into the speakers and play tunes. While very heavy (it's made for the beatings from a float trip), it operates on three AA batteries (which we never had to change) and was loud enough for all to hear when Christine had it playing in the bow. Between all our phones and the iPod, we probably had over 20 hours of music we listened to off and on over the four days of paddling. As a dad and a different generation than my team, I was very lucky that our tastes in music were fairly similar with the exception of a few rap songs. I might not have been so happy about bringing music if I had had to listen to Jay Z the whole time.

We always made it a point to turn off the music during nighttime paddling. Sound travels a long way at night and we wanted to make sure we heard every rush of water in plenty of time to avoid problems.

Can-Panion cup holders (Dick's Sporting Goods, $3 each) – Although we went with hydration tubes, there was still plenty of times we opted to drink Gatorade and other bottled drinks. Your boat's going to get very dirty and there's nothing's grosser than having your ice cold drink roll around the floorboard of a muddy canoe. These types of cup holders are designed for canoes and clip to the gunnels, putting your drink in arm's reach and keeping it out of the muck.

8 oz. spray bottles (Walgreens, $3 each) – In the summer of 2012, the Midwest was suffering with one of the worst heat waves in history. I was very nervous about baking in 104 degrees. We purchased four 8-ounce spray bottles that we carried with us during the day. Filled with plain water, we sprayed ourselves whenever we got hot. The trigger made for a good hook that we could hang on the side of the canoe, once again putting it in arm's reach and keeping it out of the muck.

Towels (Target, $4 each) – I wanted to bring towels to have something clean that we could use to wipe our face and hands and to soak in the cooler's ice water and wrap around us if we needed to cool down. While we ended up buying two sets for each paddler (one set in the canoe and a clean set on shore ready to swap out), I think I was the only person in the canoe to use mine, but even I didn't use it very much since we had the sprayers. Next time around I think I'd leave these with the Ground Crew for use during stops.

Large sponge (Lowe's, $6) – As mentioned earlier, your boat will be muddy and wet by virtue of climbing in and out plus the dripping water from your paddle. We brought a large grout sponge that we had at home and used it to wipe off the inside of the canoe and to sop up water from the bottom of the boat.

Canoe chairs (Uncle Sam's, $40 each) – Sitting on a bench seat with no back support would have killed me because of the back surgery I had had just seven months earlier. Very similar to stadium chairs, but without the arm rests (that would get in the way of paddling), these canoe chairs have two straps underneath the seat to fasten them to a canoe bench or tractor style seats. The chairs also have side strap adjustments which allow you to adjust the angle of the chair's back. I saw different types at Cabela's and Dick's Sporting Goods, but I like the padding of the chairs from Uncle Sam's. Whatever you purchase, make sure it's easily adjustable. I found myself constantly making chair adjustments to relieve a cramp or to stretch. Being able to adjust easily gives you even more flexibility in finding (and re-finding) comfortable positions.

Seat cushions (Garden Ridge, $14 each) – One thing I can guarantee you is that whatever type of boat you're in, your butt will be raw by the time you finish. Although we already had cushioned seats as part of the canoe chairs, we added seat cushions (Garden-Ridge, $18) for even more padding.

These cushions had the added benefit that they could be placed on the bottom of the canoe where we could sit on them and rest our head on the seat to nap. The only drawback to both the seat cushions and the canoe chair was that when added together they placed you very high in the canoe, potentially making the canoe tippier. For us it was well worth the trade-off since we could also go to a kneeling position if we felt like we were too unstable.

GPS (Garmin, $120) – I just had to bring my GPS. I've owned a Garmin Oregon 450 for a few years and have used it extensively while camping and hiking, often loading the tracks onto my laptop afterward. I bought a bike mount kit (Cabela's, $15) to mount my GPS in front of me on the canoe's cross bar. Although I had high hopes, it really wasn't as valuable as I thought it was going to be. While it was fun to refer to it every once in a while ("Hey look, we're going 6.1 mph."), the reality was that it's true purpose, to keep track of where we were, was already being accomplished by the mile markers which we watched going slowly past every 10 minutes. While it would have been nice to have been able to use its calculated speed and time stopped, my batteries died 20+ hours into the race and I couldn't figure out how to combine averages. Maybe it would have been different if our speed varied more than they did, but it got pretty old looking down and seeing "6 mph."

My friend Mike Claypool and his kids used their GPS for night navigation with a trail of the main channel from Kansas City to St. Charles that someone posted on the Rivermiles Forum. Mike's crew was able to see where they were relative to the channel at night to avoid wing dikes and buoys. Great approach, although I sure they still paid close attention just to make sure there wasn't some misplaced buoy in their way.

Watch (Target, $80) – One item I did use a lot was my watch. I have a Timex Ironman that I strapped next to my GPS. I didn't use it for anything except finding the time, but it was helpful to have when coordinating with the Ground Crew.

I can already hear people saying, "We are not going to bring flowered cushions with us on this race." For those I have two responses. First, unless you've done this race before, you probably don't have any idea of how a cushion or a seat or a spray bottle helps over the course of 340 miles. While we probably went overboard, my theory was that I'd rather have them and not use them, than to want them and not have them. Which leads into my second point: Walmart. Everything listed above is stocked in some form at Walmart, meaning that you're one phone call away from getting any of these items (if you have a Ground Crew). If you bring it on the river and it doesn't add value, you can always drop it off at the next checkpoint. If you decide against it beforehand, your Ground Crew can always buy it during the race.

Don't Over Think

In the spring of 1831, at the age of 22, Abraham Lincoln and friends took goods on a flatboat from Illinois all the way down the Mississippi to New Orleans. There's no picture or drawing of their boat, but I suspect like so many boats back then that made the one-way trip[13], it wasn't made of Kevlar or aluminum, it wasn't streamlined and it wasn't balanced and they probably didn't have a sophisticated hydration system, but Lincoln had the same thing going for him that you will on this race: You're going downriver.

Think of it this way. If we could take Lincoln's flatboat stuffed with goods and start it out at Kaw Point at 8 a.m. Tuesday, it's quite possible with a 3-mph current that it would pass the St. Charles finish line only 24 hours after the race ends. Not bad for simply making sure it doesn't hit anything for five days. You only have to add one more mile an hour to the speed of the current to make St. Charles in just under the 88-hour time limit.

The point is neither your boat nor your equipment has to be the fastest or the lightest; it just has to be comfortable enough to sustain you through 340 miles.

---

[13] As did most others, Lincoln and friends left the boat and walked back after delivering their wares. There was no way they could push/pole/paddle the boat back up the river.

PART VIII

COST FOR
2012 MR340 RACE

PART VIII – COST FOR THE 2012 MR340 RACE

Table 9 - 2012 Boatacious Blondes Race Cost summarizes our cost for the race. I debated whether or not to include the costs. The first time I added them up was for this book, and to say I was surprised is an understatement. But I wanted to show what we spent so you realize that there can be significant costs associated with this race and to plan accordingly. More than any one thing in this book, cost forces you to ask, "Is this piece of equipment worth it?" For us, I tempered that with what I would have been thinking if we had dropped out of the race: "Would I have bought this item now, knowing it would have prevented us from quitting?" There's no perfect answer, but I was willing to spend money on something I thought would be an additive advantage that would help us get to the finish line. That said, I also had the money (and an understanding wife) that allowed me to purchase those things. You may not be so lucky, in which case you have some tougher decisions to make than us.

Here are some cost considerations:

- When looking at the numbers, remember we had four paddlers. These numbers go down substantially the fewer paddlers you have.

- Having team t-shirts made was a great investment for both paddlers and the ground crew. Besides letting everyone know who you are, it's fun to see it in your closet years later and "remember when."

- Purchasing four canoe chairs was expensive, but for us, having adjustable back support for four days made a difference.

- Purchasing paddles was a huge investment (although they make nice holiday gifts). Lightweight used or rental paddles are available. Check around on the Rivermiles Forum.

- We completely over purchased snacks for the trip. Remember how I brought enough to feed all of Lexington on the first leg? We had 100 times that amount left over when we were done with the race. The good news was we could use them as snacks for lunch afterward, which we did almost until December.

- The Jefferson City hotel was higher because we used two hotel rooms. Look for ones that supply breakfast.

- Compression shirts were expensive but well worth the investment.

- All equipment and clothing are ready to go again. If we did it again with four people we'd be able to do it for much less.

- And finally, I'm a terrible shopper. Make you list early, figure out what you have and what you can borrow, and then take your time shopping for the rest. Almost everything on this list is on sale at one time or another (except for the week prior to the race). It's at that point you end up spending lots of money because you don't have time.

Category	Item	Total
Cash	Cash	$ 130
Cash Total		$ 130
Clothing	Sock Liners	$ 27
	Hats	$ 38
	Girl's Pants & Shirts	$ 73
	Compression Shirts	$ 140
	Team Shirts	$ 144
Clothing Total		$ 422
Entry Fee	MR340 Entry Fee ($175 @ 4)	$ 700
Entry Fee Total		$ 700
Equipment	Cupholders	$ 16
	Spot Tracker	$ 33
	Towels	$ 40
	MagLite	$ 50
	Bike Gloves	$ 56
	Flashlights & Compression Bag	$ 106
	Misc	$ 150
	PDFs	$ 153
	Canoe Chairs	$ 183
	Boat Rental	$ 350
	Paddles (3)	$ 430
Equipment Total		$ 1,567
Food	Day 2 Casey's Ice/Soda	$ 9
	Day 1 Casey's ICE/Soda	$ 12
	QT Kansas City (Last Soda before Race)	$ 14
	Day 1 Dinner Ground Crew	$ 18
	Day 1 Lunch Ground Crew	$ 18

	Day 1 Papa Jacks Pizza	$	19
	Day 2 Chipotle Dinner	$	21
	Day 4 Breakfast	$	25
	Day 2 Arbys Dinner	$	27
	Day 3 Dinner Pizza Hut	$	27
	Day 1 Wal-Mart Supplies	$	28
	Day 3 Lunch McDonalds	$	34
	Monday Breakfast	$	34
	Market Kansas City Monday Lunch	$	44
	Last Minute supplies	$	50
	Day 2 Wal-Mart Supplies	$	51
	Walmart/Sams Packaged Food	$	289
Food Total		**$**	**720**
Fuel	Pilot Boonsville	$	40
	Day 3 Breaktime	$	40
	QT Kansas City	$	53
Fuel Total		**$**	**133**
Hotels	Comfort Inn	$	97
	Baymont Inn & Suites	$	142
Hotels Total		**$**	**239**
Training	MR340 DVD	$	45
Training Total		**$**	**45**
Grand Total		**$**	**3,956**

Table 9 - 2012 Boatacious Blondes Race Cost

.

.

EPILOGUE

EPILOGUE

The Monday morning after the race I got out of my same bed, ate my same breakfast, got in my same car, drove to my same office building and sat down in my same chair in my same cubicle. "So what did you do on vacation last week?" someone asked. "Canoed in a 340-mile race on the Missouri River," I replied. "Oh, that's nice," they said. "Say, are you planning on attending the staff meeting at 11?"

That's when I realized that the MR340 Race is incomprehensible to most normal humans. If I had said I ran a marathon, they would have got it. Stayed on a beach in Florida. Got it. But by virtue of paddling 340 miles in the longest canoe and kayak race in the world, I had participated in something my co-workers may never, ever understand.

Yet I understood. And there are others who understand as well. You, by participating in this race, have set yourself apart from "normal." By attempting the MR340, you'll be joining a very small select group of men and women with a taste for adventure, having the experience of paddling one of the greatest rivers in the world.

Welcome to the club.

POSTSCRIPT

TWO BOATACIOUS BLONDES
AND KRIS' 2013 MR340 RACE

POSTSCRIPT

On Tuesday morning, 22 July 2013, a new team of blondes, now known as "Two Boatacious Blondes and Kris," climbed into that trusty Minnesota III at Kaw Point to begin another adventure on the Missouri River. Consisting of my daughter Christine (19), now an experienced MR340 racer, and her two friends new to the race, Anne (19) and Kris (19) (Kris was the non-blonde), they were out to test all that advice we laid out in this book.

Doing something once provides a single snapshot of that moment's time and place. But the Missouri River isn't a static creature day to day, much less year to year, so the MR340 is bound to be different every time. While we understood those potential changes when we wrote about our first time adventure, I was curious how different this year's race would be compared to last year's, and how those differences might affect first time racers.

My initial thought was to roll these observations from subsequent races into the main book. But after some consideration I decided I would place them in a section of their own to better illustrate what may change from year to year.

MR340 RULE CHANGES

New to 2013 was the "Reaper," a safety boat that traveled at the exact cutoff time throughout the race. The Reaper is a visible representation of the cutoff pace. By arriving at the checkpoint precisely at the cutoff time, the Reaper made it clear to paddlers and spectators which racers were DQ'd. Those who arrived after the Reaper were out.

The Reaper crew also motivated paddlers who were "on the bubble" and helped those who weren't going to make the cutoff come to terms with and digest it. The Reaper crew takes no joy in passing racers, but keeping the race on a defined schedule is a critical safety aspect. Look around every so often, especially on the first leg to Lexington when you may be finding your pace. Seeing the Reaper a few miles behind you might provide enough time to crank up your paddling as opposed to having it pass you 10 minutes away from the checkpoint.

MISSOURI RIVER CHANGES

The river was slightly lower than the previous year, but it was amazing how many sandbars were uncovered and available in 2013 when compared to 2012. In 2012, besides Hill Island, I don't think we saw a sandbar prior to Glasgow on Wednesday morning. This year, sandbars were all over the river. While the river current didn't appear to be noticeably slower, sandbar availability all along the course made catching a quick nap or taking shore breaks that much easier.

RACE STATISTICS

A part of me thought a book such as this would somehow impact DNFs. No luck. The one-third DNF percentage still applied (I can't say how many had read this book). And not only did this book have no effect on the numbers of DNFs, neither did the temperature.

As horrifically hot as the 2012 race was, the 2013 version was spectacularly mild. Staying in the low 80s during the day and mid- to upper-60s at night (cool enough to sleep in the minivan with the windows rolled up) with only a near miss of rain Tuesday afternoon, the temperature couldn't have been better for an outdoor adventure like the MR340. Imagine my surprise when the DNF percentage remained stuck in the low 30%.

Did the lower temperature reduce the overall race times? No luck there either. The average finishing time in 2013 was 70:30 (Hours:Minutes); in 2012 it was 72:17. Sure, there was a little over an hour difference, but the total percentage change was less than 2.5 %. Maybe the weather had something to do with it, but then again that variance might have been caused by water level, wind, racer entries or any number of other factors. Temperature just wasn't that big of a factor.

So, based on 2012 and 2013 results, is it okay to not worry about race temperature since it doesn't seem to have any effect on DNFs? Asking that type of question misses the key point about approaching the race. It's not about considering or ignoring one thing. It's about being prepared to address as many things as you can, as best as you can, realizing for every one you address, there's others you're not even aware of. Why didn't the heat (or lack of it) affect the DNFs? Because it is just one of a hundred things that could cause you not to finish. Heat was a factor in 2012, but being cooler in 2013 didn't eliminate exhaustion, blisters, lack of sleep, sunburn and all those others things that can also cause you to quit. Plan to manage as many discomforts as you can, knowing that depending on the year, some will be bigger challenges than others.

ACCUMULATED ADVANTAGES

Our magnificent ground crew spoiled us in 2012. Being just one phone call away from pizza, lip balm, Starbuck's Ice Coffee and anything else we could think of was an incredible advantage that played a key part of our first time finish. In 2013, I found my role reversed by sharing the Ground Crew role with Linda. Having both the paddler and Ground Crew perspectives further reinforced my belief of the critical role the Ground Crew has in helping paddlers, especially first time paddlers, finish the race.

A couple of thing we did in 2013 illustrate the power of the Ground Crew. First, using a Missouri Conservation map we packed for just such an opportunity, we drove to a number of different access points along the river to cheer the team onward. The river seems endless at times, so a quick "hi" to the paddlers along the way when they're not expecting it does wonders for their morale. Although we saw them very briefly, we could see their excitement through their upbeat paddle tempo.

In addition to surprising them with visits, we also surprised our paddlers with treats. Prior to stopping at Franklin Island Access (slightly downstream from Boonville), we stopped by the local grocery store and bought some fresh blueberries, grapes, blackberries and strawberries, which we then put into a large disposable cup for each paddler. As the ladies paddled toward the boat ramp, we waved to them to pull along the shoreline. There, without getting out of the canoe, we resupplied Anne, Christine and Kris with drinks and snacks while they ate their cool, healthy fruit treat. It was easy to do, wasted very little time and had a tremendous impact on their outlook.

The Boatacious Blondes and Kris paddled into the Noren (Jefferson City) Checkpoint at 3:00 a.m. Thursday morning, ready and raring for more (okay, Anne and Kris were ready and raring, Christine not so much). Our minivan was ready for the three girls to sleep inside (we put all the equipment we were carrying outside on the ground). After a quick discussion about continuing and a bathroom break, they hopped back in the canoe and started paddling for our next rendezvous while Linda and I repacked the van and headed down the road. While that really wasn't our plan, we had to go along if the paddlers were game. But the decision to continue not only meant repacking and heading to the next stop in the middle of the night, it meant we were about to discover the unique power of a 4:00 a.m. visit to Walmart.

The decision to continue on from Noren meant that breakfast for the Boatacious Blondes would occur in Mokane Access, not Jefferson City. The nice thing about Jefferson City is that there are lots of food places as well as 24-hour gas stations for a quick acquisition of food or drinks (especially hot coffee). Not so with Mokane. Not only are there limited places to get resupplied in the daytime (the town of Mokane has a population of 185), all such places are closed in the middle of the night. If we would have been facing a lunch or dinner, it would have been different (we had plenty of things to eat packed away in the minivan), but I remembered how much I savored waffles at the Jefferson City hotel or the Florissant Old Town Donuts and coffee at Klondike, so I knew we needed to get our paddlers something special for breakfast. With fast food not available, we stopped at the next best place – Walmart.

The Walmart Supercenter in Fulton is actually not that far off the race course. We had already visited Walmart in Kansas City (snack and drinks in preparation for the race) and in Marshall (swimming noodle for use as a bumper guard and new portable speakers to replace the ones that died), so we had a pretty good idea of what we could find. We ended up buying prepackaged cups of instant oatmeal and instant coffee, but then had to buy a small propane camping stove, propane, butane lighter and a teakettle so we could heat water for the oatmeal and instant coffee (where else but Walmart at 4:00 a.m.?). While it was irritating to buy yet another propane stove when we already have two in the garage back in St. Louis, the smiles and happiness expressed by the Boatacious Blondes as they ate a nice warm breakfast at Mokane Thursday morning more than made up for the extra stove. Walmart is truly the place to go, day or night, if there's something you need.

In 2012 we all knew that our first time finishing wasn't a sure bet. But the 2013 version of the Boatacious Blondes were a different breed. It could have been they were extremely confident because of Christine's successful finish the year before. Or maybe it was because they looked at me and thought, "If he made it, I better make it." But I believe their finishing was due primarily to their positive mental approach. Christine said it best, "This is going to suck, but it's so cool!"

It will suck, guaranteed. But the Boatacious Blondes proved once again that keeping a positive outlook and sharing that outlook with fellow paddlers is a key advantage that will get you over the inevitable rough sections of the race.

BE SAFE

The 2013 version of the Boatacious Blondes made lots of good safety decisions over the course of the race, but three instances are worth highlighting.

By using the same Minnesota III canoe that we used in 2012 but with one less paddler, Anne, Christine and Kris had ample space to sleep. And that they did on a revolving basis. I was concerned that they would keep pressing to make time, then run the chance of all wanting to sleep at the same time. Instead they set up times for each to get some quality sleep (sometimes up to two hours), being safe and making effective use of their time.

We read lots of accounts on the Rivermiles Forum about fog but didn't experience any during 2012 (probably due to the heat) and didn't see any in 2013 until Mokane on Thursday morning. There we had a ringside seat to see just what Missouri River fog is like.

We arrived at the Mokane Access Point, 20 miles downstream from Jefferson City right before sunrise, and although there were wisps of fog dotting over the river, we could see upstream and downstream very clearly. Then, in the span of 20 minutes, the fog got thicker and thicker, until finally you couldn't see anything on the river at all. We got nervous to see the river get socked in the quickly and even more so when about five fishermen launched their fishing boats into the fog. To the fishermen's credit, none went screaming into the nothingness, but it was pretty amazing how fast they were swallowed up by the fog as they slowly rumbled away.

But where were our paddlers? We expected them to arrive around 7:30 a.m., but it was impossible to tell how bad the fog was upstream, and it would have been hard for them to pull over knowing that there was hot coffee and oatmeal were waiting for them downstream. Turns out they had things well under control. As they saw the fog move in, they moved closer to shore so they had a place to duck in if it got too thick. When it reached that point where they couldn't see as well as they thought they should, they pulled in behind a wing dike then beckoned over another paddler to do the same. There they napped and waited until the fog lifted an hour or so later.

It's easy for me to sit in my nice comfy armchair and think, "I'd be smart enough to do that." It's another thing to be on the river with minimal sleep, trying to break 65 hours, and have coffee and oatmeal waiting for you 20 minutes away, and make that same decision. The decision they made is the one you need to be ready to make, knowing the right decision won't necessarily be easy or clear cut.

Having been part of the 2012 convoy out of Klondike with two solo paddlers, Christine was very much in tune with the concept of "paddle like a girl" and connecting up with other racers, especially solo paddlers. It was fun to hear them talk at a checkpoint about who they paddled with along the previous section. As with their fog experience, it's tempting to keep pressing and not slow down just a little bit to keep company with that solo paddler at 2:00 a.m. upstream from Jefferson City, but knowing the power of camaraderie and the safety factor it brings, the Boatacious Blondes did a good job in 2013 being aware of others and using teamwork to both their and their fellow racers' advantage.

ENDURE

Group dynamics are a funny thing. I've been a part of groups that should have clicked and didn't, and I have been part of groups that by all rights had no business doing what we were doing yet did great. The 2013 Boatacious Blondes were very special young ladies whose adventure spirit showed brightly during the race. But what made these young women great paddlers was their teamwork. Besides cheering each other on, they were each other's watchful eyes. Have you been drinking enough liquids? Do you need a quick nap? Are you okay steering? It's not often you'll see teams with that level of trust and communication.

CLOCK MANAGEMENT

Our 2012 race involved staying in the 300-foot channel as much as possible, preferably in the center section. As you can imagine, staying dead in the center isn't an exact science, but I felt we did a good job making the most of the current by staying true to the channel. When I provided "staying in the channel" instructions to the team this time around, I really didn't talk about using the GPS as a true navigation instrument. I only suggested they look at it every so often to get an idea of their average pace so they could better project checkpoint arrivals.

I was somewhat surprised, then, when Christine and Kris talked about how religious Anne was in watching the GPS to find the right spot in the river to maximize their speed. After querying Anne, I found out to the paddlers increased their speed anywhere from 0.5 to 0.75 mph just by making small 20- to 30-feet location adjustments in the channel. Anne kept an eye on the GPS speed and could tell by the drop in speed if they were moving outside the fastest water.

Interesting concept, but I'm not sure I fully appreciated her strategy until I paddled with two friends in the "Race to the Dome" in September 2013. Sure enough, we could see a substantial speed difference just by making slight adjustments in our canoe's position in the channel. In the 2012 MR340, I would have ranked my GPS in the "nice to have" category, but after hearing and seeing the difference it can make, I now would place it in the "must have" category. Anything that gets you another 0.5 mph without much effort is a good deal.

Christine was surprised at how many paddlers hugged the shore during the first section of the race. It's probably a combination of being uncomfortable in a huge river like the Missouri along with the urge to be close to everyone else who happens to be near the shore. Be aware that the closer to shore you are, the less "free" speed you get from the river.

One other thing the 2013 Boatacious Blondes did that made them more efficient was to alternate eating times. During our race, we all stopped to snack, and in doing so spent a fair amount of time drifting. Anne, Christine and Kris alternated who ate so there were always two people paddling at any given time. It may not seem like much, but slowing down so everyone can eat at the same time adds up over the course of a 340-mile race.

The 2013 Boatacious Blondes did a magnificent job of clock management. Their goal was to break 65 hours, and they knew that in order to finish in that time meant they couldn't spend much time on shore. Table 10 - Boatacious Blondes and Kris's 2013 Checkpoint Times shows just how well they did at each checkpoint.

Checkpoint	Checkpoint Times		Time on River	Time on Shore	
				Awake	Sleep
Kaw Point Out	Tues.	8:00 AM			
Lexington In	Tues.	4:20 PM	8:20		
Lexington Out	Tues.	4:35 PM		0:15	
Waverly In	Tues.	8:25 PM	3:50		
Waverly Out	Tues.	8:45 PM		0:20	
Miami In	Wed.	2:05 AM	5:20		
Miami Out	Wed.	2:50 AM		0:45	
Glasgow In	Wed.	9:30 AM	6:40		
Glasgow Out	Wed.	11:30 AM		0:30	1:30
Franklin Isl.* In	Wed.	--			
Franklin Isl* Out	Wed.	--		0:10	
Katfish Katy's In	Wed.	7:45 PM	8:15		
Katfish Katy's Out	Wed.	8:15 PM		0:30	
Jeff. City In	Thurs.	3:00 AM	6:45		
Jeff. City Out	Thurs.	3:45 AM		0:45	
Mokane* In	Thurs.				
Mokane* Out	Thurs.			0:15	2:00
Hermann In	Thurs.	3:45 PM	9:45		
Hermann Out	Thurs.	4:10 PM		0:25	
Klondike In	Thurs.	11:15 PM	7:05		
Klondike Out	Thurs.	11:40 PM		0:25	
St Charles In	Fri.	3:46 AM	4:06		
* not a checkpoint	Total Time:		60:06	4:10	3:30

Table 10 - Boatacious Blondes and Kris's 2013 Checkpoint Times

Compared to 2012, they reduced their shore time by nine hours. This was achieved in large part by sleeping in the canoe, which reduced their sleeping time on shore by more than 7 hours.

As you can see from Table 10, the Boatacious Blondes' on-shore turnaround time was very fast. Their speed getting through the checkpoints was in large part due to what they did in the boat. They ate, drank and pottied prior to, instead of at, the checkpoints. We as Ground Crew did our part, having the minivan set up for sleeping so all they had to do was get out of the boat, hop in the van and close their eyes. Of course this didn't happen at every stop; they still took a few minutes to eat hamburgers in Miami and hot oatmeal at Mokane, but even there they had one eye on the food and the other on the clock.

It's interesting to consider what minimizing shore time meant in terms of overall race time. In 2012 we completed the race in just over 77 hours, with about 17 hours of race time spent on shore. In 2013, Anne, Christine and Kris completed the race in 67:46 with their on-shore time around 7 hours, 40 minutes. That meant they actually paddled only an hour or so faster than we did the year before. The rest of the time was gained by fast turnarounds on land. Minimizing shore time is an easy way to gain time, but it's important to remember that it's the things you do in the boat prior to the checkpoint that minimizes your time on shore.

EQUIPMENT

Having just written a book about equipment, we had packing for the race down pat. But I realized, after we did all the packing, that Anne, Christine and Kris didn't necessarily know the contents or purpose of everything we packed. When doing it again, I would spend much more time with the team talking about what's in what bag, and why it's there.

When preparing for the 2012 race, I read a thread on Rivermiles about bringing goggles or safety glass along to keep bugs out of your eyes while paddling at night. I thought that would be a pretty strange situation, so I didn't bother to pack anything, and that year we had absolutely no problems with bugs either on or off the water. Then came 2013.

Apparently bugs will hatch all at once along the river, and depending on when you go, you might see billions or none at all. Unfortunately, 2013 was the year of billions. Poor Kris sat in the bow of the canoe with the hood of her sweatshirt tied tightly around her face, sunglasses on, in the middle of the night, buried by bugs. Safety Boat crews reported that many times they couldn't see anything except a wall of bugs when they showed the spotlight on the river. Clear safety glasses along with a dust mask might be a worthwhile investment just in case the race coincides with a bug infestation.

Both Anne and Kris had iPhones, so prior to the race everyone loaded the "Find Friends" app and "friended" each other so we could keep track of the boat's location. During the race, we switched phones in and out of the boat, charging the one we took from the boat. There are two things to consider when taking this approach. First, Anne had songs loaded on her phone, so sometimes in the middle of the day they reach for a song set only to realize it was on shore charging. It might have been worthwhile to load all the songs on an iPod that could be charged at night. The second consideration was lack of cell coverage. We had very good cell coverage using Verizon until downstream from Jefferson City. From there almost until Washington, coverage was very spotty. There's not much you can do in those situations. Just don't be lulled into thinking you'll always know where you or your Ground Crew are all the time. Paddlers should have maps, and Ground Crews should keep a running estimated time of arrival based on boat speed just in case cell coverage drops out upstream from the checkpoint.

COST FOR THE MR340 RACE

The good news is it's cheaper the second time around. There's not much you can do about hotels, food and gas, but there wasn't much equipment we had to buy for 2013.

Once we figured out that Ellen wasn't going to make this year's race, I made a quick call to Josh Pennington who rented the Minnesota III to us in 2012. "You're more than welcome to rent the canoe like you did last year," Josh said, "but I'd also be willing to sell it if you're interested."

Hmmmmm...

As I pondered his offer, I went onto the Rivermiles Buy/Sell/Trade Forum to see what other type of boats were available. And there I made a discovery. Unlike cars, which can lose a big chunk of value driving off the dealer's lot, most canoes and kayaks used for races such as the MR340 tend to hold their value for a fairly long time (barring a buoy collision). This means that if you have the money (and an understanding spouse), you could purchase the boat of your choice prior to the race, participate in the race, then sell the boat for somewhere close to what you paid.[14] While buying ties up a larger amount of money than renting, you now have time with the exact boat you'll use for the race as opposed to paddling it for the first time on race day.

The 2013 MR340 Race was an event of a lifetime for Anne, Christine and Kris. John Wooden, the famous college basketball coach, once said, "Sports do not build character. They reveal it." I think the same is true with the MR340. It's brutal, it's long, and there are lots of opportunities not to finish, but it's also a magnificent way to challenge yourself in a unique manner and to share in that challenge with some great people. Your MR340 adventure may be similar to the Boatacious Blondes, but in many ways, just like the river, it'll be unique each and every time you race.

We'll see you at the finish.

---

[14] **Of course assuming you did your homework and didn't overpay.**

Stephen, Linda, Robert, Ellen, Christine and Claire Jackson

ACKNOWLEDGMENTS

Grateful acknowledgment is made to our superb book reviewers: Scott Mansker, Steve Schnarr, Brett Dufur, Mike Claypool and Bob Linhares; and to my editor, Megan Linhares, and cover designer, Christopher Lightner.

Their time and insight was greatly appreciated.

CONNECT WITH US ONLINE

Author Website: http://www.stephencjackson.com